AND STILL HE SPEAKS

Other Books by Edward L. R. Elson

ONE MOMENT WITH GOD
AMERICA'S SPIRITUAL RECOVERY

EDWARD L. R. ELSON

And Still He Speaks
THE WORDS OF THE RISEN CHRIST

FLEMING H. REVELL COMPANY

Scripture references marked RSV are from the *Revised Standard Version of the Bible,* copyrighted 1946 and 1952 by the division of Christian Education, National Council of Churches, and are used by permission.

"The White Presence" from *God and the Golden Rule* by Joseph Fort Newton is reprinted by permission of Appleton-Century-Crofts, Inc.

TO THE TWO DAVIDS IN MY LIFE

DAVID C. SHIPLEY

AND

DAVID EDWARD ELSON

Preface

THE CENTRAL FACT of Christian history is the resurrection of Jesus Christ; it is the great fact on which all else turns. On Easter morning the Jesus of history emerged from the tomb to become the living Christ of the ages. In the early church, the resurrection of Jesus was the one thing a Christian could not deny and remain a Christian. Authentic Christianity is anchored on this truth.

To the followers of Jesus, this resurrection was the proof that He was the Christ, the Messiah of God. They followed Him not because He taught an ethical code, although He had such a code. Nor did the early church merely assert a vague, ephemeral doctrine of immortality in common with other great religions. The earliest disciples spoke of their resurrected Lord as a unique, vivid, identifiable, communicating Person, at once identical with the Person with whom they had walked. His indubitable presence was proof of their redemption. His resurrection was the mighty act of God. In Jesus, God had revealed His nature to man. God had come among men to allow men to see Him. He was the "image of the invisible God," as Paul wrote to the Colossians. In Him God had demonstrated the power of goodness over evil. The life, the teaching, the suffering and the death of our Lord Jesus Christ derive their meaning from the transcendent truth of the resurrection. This was and is authentic Christianity.

For forty days and forty nights the Lord of the disciples broke in upon them, made Himself known beyond all doubt. He came to individuals, to small groups, and at least once to a crowd of five hundred, in eleven recorded appearances. "And many other signs truly did Jesus in the presence of his disciples, which are not written in this book: But these are written, that ye might believe that Jesus is the Christ, the Son of God; and that believing ye might have life through his name" (John 20:30, 31).

So the resurrected Lord came to His followers under many circumstances in many different places. Then one day He went out of the sight of some in order to be near His followers forever.

Christian scholars throughout the ages, liberal and conservative, have been probing all aspects of the subject. Some of them have possessed massive minds and have been thoroughly adept in scientific research. Although I am acquainted with their literature, this monograph is more concerned with the reality of the resurrection in the experience of the church than with the technical aspects. Yet it is well to note that such a precise scholar as Bishop B. F. Westcott, after long philosophic, scientific and historical research, concludes, "If now, we give fair weight to all these considerations—to the personal attestation of the fact by the apostles, to the circumstances under which Paul was led to proclaim it, to its relation to Christ's whole work, to the transformation which it effected in the opinions and conduct of the first disciples, to its continuous efficacy in life—I find no reason to modify what I have said elsewhere, that, taking all the evidence together, there is no single historical incident better or more variously supported than the Resurrection of Christ." [1] The dependable scholar, Alfred Edersheim, also concludes his treatment of the subject by declaring that the resurrection of Jesus Christ unquestionably may be pronounced the best-established fact in history.[2]

More recently, Richard R. Niebuhr of the Harvard Divinity School faculty, in a significant work has pointed out, among other things, that the rejection of the resurrection would be the denial of historical continuity. The fact of the resurrection and the experience of the disciples with that fact is the only way history can have valid meaning. He maintains that "the resurrection of Christ does not violate Nature but only death. It epitomizes the original creativity that informs all history and underlies every conception of Nature. The resurrection of Jesus

Christ, considered from the point of view of the historical events in whose midst it transpires, occupies a privileged position." Then he concludes, "As we look back through the church's memory, we see that they were constrained to recognize a Lord greater than death who reigned in their own history. From such recognition both judgment and hope flow for those who are able to recognize and who in the act of recognition witness to the faithfulness of God." [3]

While our purpose here is not to marshal the conclusions of the scholars so much as to witness to the reality of the resurrection, yet I believe it important for Christians to know and to declare that the resurrection as historic fact, and as a reality in the life of the church, rests on a secure intellectual foundation. The rejection of the resurrection is not a mark of superior wisdom or of a higher intellect. Some minds cannot be convinced by any evidence whatsoever; but that is no evidence of their superiority. The central fact of Christian history and experience belongs where it has always been, in the central place. And it is kept there by all the proper laws of evidence and the recurrent corroboration of Christian experience. The reality of the living Christ derived from the resurrection certitude is the authentic and essential element in Christian worship, Christian belief and Christian fellowship.

In the classical tradition of the church, Easter Eve concludes the forty-day period called Lent, when the teachings and the Passion of our Lord are emphasized. Eastertide embraces the period from Easter Sunday through Ascension Day. A proper commemoration of the resurrection therefore includes a protracted period of the year. The reasons for the disappearance of the observance of the Christian Year at the time of the Reformation do not now have the same force or validity, as the Church of Scotland pointed out in the preface to its *Prayers for the Christian Year*. In the Reformed and Evangelical tradition, much attention is now given to the pre-Easter season. Holy Week is now a period of intense spiritual discipline. Good Friday is widely commemorated with services devoted to the words from the cross. Not so much attention is given to the post-Easter season, to the words *after* the cross. Yet it is clear from history and experience that this ought to be the season with the really triumphant accent.

In some fresh way, year after year, we ought to deal with the after-Easter aspects of the record. These chapters represent the substance of one such effort. My congregation in the National Presbyterian Church has evoked this series. To them I am indebted for constant inspiration and increasing affection. Some of the material has been used at convocations of the clergy and at several theological schools across the country. It is our hope that these pages will strengthen the faith and quicken the devotion of Christians at every level of spiritual perception.

Acknowledgment

I AM INDEBTED to the late minister and professor, Dr. Doremus A. Hayes, who, after retiring from the chair of New Testament Interpretation in the Garrett Biblical Institute, spent part of each year in La Jolla, California, and attended the Presbyterian Church of which I was then pastor. During this period we had many long and rewarding talks together, and it was during this period that Dr. Hayes published his volume, *The Resurrection Fact*. I had already plunged into the study of the resurrection and my interest has deepened with the passing of the years. No other person has contributed so much to the development of my own views as Doremus A. Hayes. For his friendship and his works I am profoundly grateful.

Contents

AND STILL HE SPEAKS

1 The Word of Confirmation

"Jesus saith unto her, Mary. . . ." (*John 20:16*)

GREAT MEN COME and go in history. They make their impact. They achieve eminence and the world acclaims them. Their biographers interpret them. When they are gone their memorials are erected.

Not so with Jesus of Nazareth. Other men appeared and disappeared, but Jesus came upon the stage and has remained there, eternally the same.

Men's beliefs about Jesus and their understanding of Him may change from time to time, yet He does not change. Jesus Christ is God's Word to man. God's forgiveness, God's mercy, God's healing, God's presence do not change. He is forever alive, forever available.

AND STILL HE SPEAKS

There was only one day when Jesus Christ was out of touch with our life; that was the Saturday between the crucifixion on Friday and the resurrection on Sunday. It was the resurrection that made all the difference. It was the resurrection which transformed Him from a transitory leader to a permanent presence. On the third day, He arose. What He was then He is eternally. What He was to the first disciples He may be to us. He is history's perpetual contemporary.

On the resurrection morning when He renewed His fellowship with His disciples, His first word was not spoken to a congregation, nor to His family, nor to the apostolic band. It was spoken to a forlorn and solitary woman searching an empty tomb. Mary Magdalene had watched the cruel drama on Calvary. When Jesus cried, "It is finished," all the luster and glory of her life had fled.

In the middle of the night, long before daybreak on the first day of the week she threaded her way through the paths toward the tomb where the body of Jesus had been placed. In deep despair she walked over the hill called Olivet down into the Valley of Kidron, through the bypasses of the little olive orchard, the Garden of Gethsemane, rounding the northeast corner of the city wall, past the north side of the Damascus Gate. Mary looked up at the shadowy skull-shaped hill, and came at length to Joseph's blooming garden. With spices and perfume in her hand, she was intent upon anointing the body.

When Mary reached the Garden, a soft radiance shone from the tomb. The stone had been rolled away; the grave was vacated.

So amazed was she by the discovery that the tomb was empty that she ran for Peter and John. She found them and announced the startling news that the sepulcher was empty. They immediately dashed off in the direction of Joseph's garden. Mary was so exhausted from her experience at the tomb that the two disciples in their fresh vigor first outwalked and then outran her.

When at length she came back panting to the tomb, the two men were already inside making a careful inspection. Mary sat down by the doorway to compose herself. Soon Peter and John moved out briskly, their faces white with amazement. They passed the woman without a word of greeting or thanks for her kind message. At the mouth of the tomb, sitting in her solitude and desolation, Mary burst into a flood of tears. Poor stricken soul! What agony was hers. If the Master had lived—if the Master had lived He would not have ignored her as did these two men. He was the very soul of courtesy. No one had treated her as He had. No one would ever treat her so again. With a heart overburdened with sorrow, she stooped again to look into the vacant tomb. The body was not there. That

was a certainty. Her Lord was not in that sepulcher.

Thrilled by the sight of the empty tomb and by its
promises, Peter and John had gone away without shar-
ing with Mary their perplexities, surmises and great ex-
pectations. As she looked again into the tomb she was
greeted by two messengers. In her sorrow she heard one
of them say, "Woman, why weepest thou?" Her heart
leaped. She made quick response: "Because they have
taken away my Lord, and I know not where they have
laid him." [1]

As Peter and John fled from the scene it occurred to
her to call out to them, but as she turned to look after
the unheeding apostles she saw a man standing by, whose
dress resembled the gardener's. If he were in charge of
this garden and this grave, he was up very early in the
morning. Perhaps she thought of him as an intruder
when he said, "Woman, why weepest thou? whom seek-
est thou?" She pointed to the empty tomb and with
choking grief implored, "Sir, if thou have borne him
hence, tell me where thou hast laid him, and I will take
him away." [2] Her only desire was to find that body, that
she might anoint it and care for it—the last possible loving act she could perform. Then the man spoke to her
the word that transformed her life, that recovered for
her the faded radiance and brought back the bloom of
hope and faith. The word she heard was simply—
"Mary!"—and it was the voice of Jesus Himself. That

22

familiar voice speaking her name in the way only Jesus could speak it and with the accent she had heard so often was enough for her. A great reality swept over her. The sense of her Lord's presence with her surged through her being. That voice had spoken to her before and she was made alive. Hearing that voice made her alive again. When the thrill and wonder of it all seemed more than she could bear, she gasped a halting salutation, "Rabboni!" *"Master!"*

Mary's agony had been very great. Her joy now was unbounded. He had disappeared from her view and was lost, she thought, forever. "I never must have that experience again. I never must lose Him out of my sight. No one shall ever steal Him away again. I will cling to Him. I will hold Him fast forever."

In an instant, it all went through her mind. The love of her whole being surged into her face in a look of great desire, a desire for immediate apprehension and continuous personal possession. She would hold Him fast forever. There must be no more separations, no more Fridays like the last, no more entombments. She would cling to Him forever.

Jesus saw all this and said, in effect, "Touch me not. I am to be with you forever, even as you desire, but not in this form. I must ascend to the Father. Go tell my brethren that and remind them that I ascend unto my Father, your Father, my God and your God. And I will come again and be with them to the end of the age." [3]

23

Mary had heard that voice before. There was no mistaking it. Her faith was now made sure. The voice conveyed the confirming word . . . the voice that would echo down the ages, the voice of the Lord Jesus Christ who would abide with stricken souls forever.

It was characteristic of Jesus to draw people close to Him. A woman pushed through the crowd and touched the hem of His garment and strength flowed into her at that touch. Another who had been forgiven kissed His feet and wiped them with her loosened hair. Jesus did not reject close association with people nor resent their touching Him. He was always available to people. All kinds of people had access to Him.

And so it was after the resurrection. We read later that other women "took hold of his feet and worshiped him" [4] and He did not protest. In the evening of the day of resurrection He invited the disciples to assure themselves: "It is I myself; handle me, and see." [5] To Thomas on the following Sunday He said, "Reach hither thy hand, and thrust it into my side." [6] He did not shrink from the touch of His disciples. He encouraged it. But after identifying Himself He admonished Mary, "Touch me not." Could it be that her desire to possess Him, to hold Him, was so overpowering as to crowd out a purer faith and trust, and that the resurrected Lord wanted to implant in her a surer, more abiding faith? She seemed unwilling to trust Him out of her sight again, yet the lesson she had to learn was that she could not always keep Him in sight or "in hand." "Touch me not," He said.

But the voice echoed clear and sure. He spoke the word that brought light and life back to her dead spirit. Mary too had died on Friday. For Mary too it was resurrection morning. She hurried to the disciples saying words like these: "I have *seen* the Lord. I have been with him; I have heard him speak; he has sent me to you." [7] "Come—see."

Years before, Jesus had spoken Mary's name and it had brought new life to her. She was a woman of Magdala, a town of great distinction. She had been admitted to the intimacy of Jesus' life. Mary had been an afflicted woman to whom the Master had brought health. It is said of her that she possessed seven devils; in the Gospels this meant a disease to be healed and not a crime to be forgiven. Its victims were to be pitied—not blamed. Perhaps Mary Magdalene once had some psychotic symptoms. No doubt she was possessed of an intense introspection, given to depression and melancholy. Once her spirits had been shattered. Then Jesus met her and healed her—her life had been made whole. In abiding gratitude for the great gift of health and new purpose, Mary followed Jesus and ministered to Him and with Him.

Luke names Mary first among the women, implying perhaps that she was the most influential. If she had suffered a sevenfold illness, she may have been restored

to sevenfold energy of character and a sevenfold endow-
ment of spirit. She was lovable, gentle and faithful.
The Gospels do not mention her personal beauty but
they do speak of her gratitude, her devotion and her
zeal.

Mary of Magdala followed Jesus across Galilee, thrilling at His words and works, then trembled at the grow-
ing hostility of the crowd. She saw Him arrested; she
saw Him tried; she heard the sentence. She saw Him
lashed. She saw that crown of thorns jabbed into His
noble brow. She followed Him up Calvary. She saw nails
bite into the hands which once lifted her. She saw a
spear thrust far into the heart that had beat with hers.
She heard Him say, "It is finished."

Standing beneath the cross Mary supported the other
Mary, the stricken mother, and helped John lead her
away at the end. Then, in the middle of the night on
the first day of the week, she returned with spices for the
body of her Master. All her hopes and life itself had been
interred with Jesus in that tomb. Gloom and despair had
settled over her until the Easter sequel when this confirming word broke upon her with the light of a new
creation.

The man Mary met in the Garden that dawn spoke
just one word—"Mary!" That was enough. That was
her own name. Jesus meant everything to her. Mary was
Mary only with Jesus. The real Mary, the whole Mary,

the cleansed Mary, the Mary of self-respect, of devotion and zeal returned with that word spoken by her Lord. Nobody could say "Mary" as Jesus could. That word was antiseptic; that word was healing; that word was forgiving; that word was full of life; that word was a word of love spoken by the deathless Lover of all.

The Lord of the resurrection morning was truly the one whom she had known in the days before Good Friday. There was about Him no criticism nor censorship. There was only kindness and love. Unlike the disciples, she had nothing to go on in life if the Kingdom of the Master were abandoned. She could not lose herself in preaching or business or farming. To Mary, life was Jesus Himself. Perhaps this is why He came first to her. That word spoken in the dawn of the first Easter meant victory—victory in her own life, and victory for the cause of her Lord. His aliveness meant her own aliveness. It gave her power. For her prayer had been answered and always would be answered. The answer to prayer henceforth would be the presence of her Lord who said, "Mary!"

When she heard her name, she then called out His name. At first she had addressed the stranger in simple courtesy saying, "Sir, if thou have borne him hence, tell me. . . ." But now in a moment of realization she uses the higher term of intimacy and says, "Rabboni."

27

That is to say, "Master, my Master . . . for ever and ever."

The first word of the risen Lord was this word of identification spoken to a disconsolate woman. As Jesus spoke to her the word of confirmation, so He comes to us and speaks to each of us His confirming word. He speaks the message each of us understands. It is in our own personal experience that we come to know the living Christ. He calls us by name. He knows us through and through. He who understood what was in man long ago understands us now. He pursues us, however far we may wander; with quenchless love He reaches after us. What He was to Mary that morning He may be to you this very hour.

Has He spoken your name? Has He spoken your name in forgiveness and love and victory? When you have opened your life to Him, He comes into your life. He comes speaking your language. He comes in your own terms. He numbers you even now among His very own.

When Easter dawn has really broken in upon your life; when you hear him say, "Mary — John — Andrew — Ruth — David — Thomas — Joseph — Edward — Sarah — Helen —" *your* name, the word that confirms *your* faith—then the risen Lord comes not as a dim figure in ancient history, not as a subject of medieval theology, not as an image in stained glass, but He comes to you as the single, unique being you are; nearer than father or mother, nearer than sister or brother, nearer than hands or feet, closer than breathing—the very life of your being. When you identify Him as surely you will, when you claim Him as He claims you, then in wonder and unutterable joy you say with Mary of old, "Rabboni— Master—my Master."

2 The Word of Salutation

"Peace be unto you." (John 20:19)

It was sunday evening. A group of men and women, still shuddering at the horrible thing they had witnessed on Friday but excited by reports and experiences during the first hours of the new week, assembled in the large room where the Last Supper had been celebrated. Here they had listened to the last address of Jesus and heard their Lord pray for Himself, for them and for the world. Here everything reminded them of Jesus.

In this familiar rendezvous the disciples had assembled hastily. Other men and women who had followed Jesus joined the apostolic band.[1] Everybody was talking about the events of the day. Several spoke of the empty tomb. There were comments about the undisturbed grave clothes. Peter said he had had a personal interview with the risen Lord that afternoon.[2] Cleopas and his companion recited their experiences on the Emmaus road and the identification which came as they dined together. They reported that while they were eating He was with them. There was no question of identity. Before they had finished He disappeared. The episode was so thrilling they hurried back to Jerusalem and to this place, hoping to tell their friends. And here they all were with their amazing stories. Thus secure behind a bolted door, the disciples excitedly exchanged accounts and assessed the reports.

As they talked a sudden hush fell on the little company; there was a new Presence in the room. Someone else had entered. All eyes were fixed on Him. They were speechless, in mixed awe and hope. Clearly and unmistakably He said, "Peace be unto you." This was the customary greeting. From this Person to these persons it meant peace to heart and conscience. It was electrifying. There was Christ before their very eyes, so obviously and undeniably that their incredulity was gone, their doubts banished. The impossible had become real in their experience of the moment.

Nothing like this had ever happened before, anywhere, at any time. Nobody had seen a figure like this. This was the resurrected Lord in the beauty of His divine majesty and power. This was the Jesus of the crucifixion whose mutilated body, with gaping wounds in hands and feet and side, had been laid in the tomb. Sure enough! The marks of Calvary were upon Him. But they were now only scars of identification. This was the same voice, the face, the same manner, the same *Person* they had known.

In their confusion and panic Jesus spoke another word: "See my hands and feet, that it is I myself; handle me, and see; for a spirit has not flesh and bones as you see that I have." [3] As they pondered His words He asked for food. Then they presented Him with a broiled fish and He ate it before them. The Gospels say that then He "opened their minds to understand the scriptures" and the disciples "were glad when they saw their Lord." They could not doubt the testimony of their own senses. One by one they recovered from their fear. Into blanched cheeks color returned. Panic turned into confidence. Frenzy and fright became faith. An ecstatic joy possessed them. They were made new as only divine reality can make men new.

During the following week the word got around that the disciples had "seen the Lord." But Thomas, who had not been with them on Sunday evening, said, "Unless I see in his hands the print of the nails, and place my finger in the mark of the nails, and place my hand in his side, I will not believe." [4] Thomas had little hope of ever believing in the resurrection. He did not say, "*When* I see . . . I shall believe." He said, "*Unless* I see . . . I shall not believe." He does not believe *he* will ever see Jesus, no matter what others may say. He is determined in his skeptical, dejected stubbornness.

Every other disciple in Jerusalem may believe these stories, but to Thomas they looked more like credulity than faith. There was no disloyalty in these questions. All of the disciples had been disloyal. They are too easily satisfied now. Thomas wanted the facts; he would not believe without sufficient reason. He wants the slowest of all senses—touch—to confirm the report. Barricaded behind stubbornness and skepticism he declares, "Unless I see in his hands . . . and place my finger in the mark of the nails, and place my hand in his side, I will not believe."

In the days of that first week Thomas lugged his doubts about with him, but he remained in the circle of the disciples. Maybe this was a wistful seeking; maybe only a defiance of the others. Or was Thomas expecting to disprove the disciples' reports and confirm his own position? John Calvin wrote that "Thomas' stubbornness is surprising, indeed monstrous. He is not only stubborn but also arrogant and insulting toward Christ." Whatever the speculations about his attitude, it is clear that Thomas wanted more evidence or he would not believe.

One week later the disciples, including Thomas, were assembled in the same familiar room. One thrilling experience after another was making more vivid and strong the resurrection conviction of the disciples. They braced each other in this meeting. Insight and understanding found illumination and confirmation as they talked together. While the door was securely bolted, as it had been on the preceding Sunday, Jesus was seen standing in the room. To the disciples He speaks the familiar salutation, "Peace be with you." Then in an act of great condescension and forgiveness He turned to Thomas and said, "Put your finger here, and see my hands; and put out your hand, and place it in my side; do not be faithless, but believing." [5] Not one demand remains unfulfilled. Not a single specification goes unmet. Nor does the Resurrected One propose a single counter requirement. He makes only one request, "Do not be faithless, but believing."

Overcome by shame, Thomas foregoes the conditions he had set down when he spoke to the disciples. He believes before he touches the risen Lord. In Thomas there is adoration, praise and thanksgiving. Waiving the privilege of validation by touch, he calls out, "My Lord and my God." It is God Himself who confronts Thomas. The appearance of Jesus is, for Thomas, an encounter with the living God. He not only recovered the Jesus whom he saw brutally put to death, but his God had come back into his life. He was ready to worship Him forever. The divine mediation was now with the risen Christ who is at once identical with the Jesus he had known. "My Lord and my God," Thomas shouted. His life was transformed. The risen Christ had come into his life as a living Person communicating with the living person, Thomas.

In this hour Thomas asked no questions about how it all happened. What kind of body this was, he seemed not to care. Jesus was absolute, and unmistakable in His identity. He got through to Thomas in the terms of personality which Thomas could understand. The famed German teacher Dr. Schlatter has written, "He remains the same and yet does not return to the former mode of life, but has become new. He controls space, as we do not control it; He is here and there as He wills. He passes through what is impenetrable for us and therefore stands in an altogether different relationship to our nature than we do. And yet He remains a bodily being, and what He had in His body before dying continues to live in Him. We face a miracle which is completely unfathomable for us."

Only in terms of miracle can this be understood. That the disciples believed beyond a shadow of a doubt that their Lord arose and became identifiable in terms of personality is one of the best authenticated facts in history. The living Christ was free from the limitations and inhibitions of the flesh and human mortality. He could assume flesh and bones, but the life pulsating through the familiar form is not the life of the blood but of a higher existence.

So Jesus speaks His word of salutation, "Peace be with you!" Men know Him and are made new by His presence.

On the resurrection day He came to a group. And that

is the way He comes to us. He promised to be real in groups. He keeps His promise. Where two or three (or two or three thousand) are gathered together in His name He is present. The mystics and the Quakers have taught us that when people are gathered together in faith, even though in silence, there is a plus factor in the group which is greater than the sum total of its parts. He comes today as He did yesterday—out of the everywhere as a Person to persons—in the here and now.

It is harder to disprove the reality of the risen Lord than to prove it. The personal experiences of the disciples and the honesty and accuracy of their reports have been authenticated as historic facts by the most thoroughgoing investigations of historians.

The reality of the resurrection has been scientifically established as authentically as scientific methodology can be applied to human personality.

How would you proceed to disprove the resurrection reality by the scientific method? It would be necessary to find a company of people who knew the mind, the heart, the temperament, the very being of Jesus and who trusted in Him. Then such a company should be assembled in the mood of expectancy, anticipation and spiritual sensitiveness. They should be convened "in His name" inviting and "expecting" His presence. They should do this time after time, meeting all these conditions. They should be followers of Jesus, knowing His mind, His heart, His personality, and be gathered "in

His name." He promised to be where such people assemble in His name. Suppose these conditions were met and the experiment were performed many, many times and it was discovered that the living Christ "did not come," that He was uniformly absent. Then it must be concluded that the report of the resurrection reality had been proved a fraud.

But what has happened when this experiment has in actual experience taken place? Whenever sincere followers of Jesus have gathered in His name, in the mood of invitation, of anticipation, and expectancy—whenever hearts and minds and emotions have been in tune—He has broken in upon men and women, out of the everywhere into conscious, describable, fellowship—as a living Person, vivid and identifiable to other persons.

Wherever groups have gathered in His name and whenever they have met these conditions, He has come—in study group, in prayer meeting, in church service. What He was that first Easter He is today—a permanent Presence.

Again, let us note that the Sunday evening encounters of the disciples with the risen Christ suggest that Jesus frequently comes as a vivid reality in familiar, homey places. He is not limited as to where He may be met or when He may break in, but habitual association of a place with His personality and presence makes that place a sanctuary of the soul where the Lord may be found.

That lesson comes out of the Upper Room. Here the

Last Supper had been commemorated. Here the lesson of humility was taught when the Master washed the disciples' feet. Here they heard His farewell address and departing prayer for Himself, for them and for the world. Here they must have foregathered many times in prayer and fellowship, in banquet, fun and rest. For some it was a complete home; for all of them, a home for the soul. It was in this place on a later day that they were all filled with the Holy Spirit and empowered for their world mission.

So He comes to us in familiar places. For four years of college, every Monday evening, I met with a group of classmates for prayer, Bible study and personal testimony. We shared with each other our experiences as we walked with Christ. But as we talked and prayed and waited, He came in the midst of that group of college students as a vivid, glowing reality. No one who had such experiences with the living Christ could be irreverent or sacrilegious in that place. He was so real in that topmost room of that old college building that it became a sanctuary of His presence—and for me and a hundred others remains so today.

During a pastorate in La Jolla, California, I acquired the habit of having my daily devotions as I walked alone along the world-famed "Coast Walk" on the jagged shores overlooking the turquoise waters of the bay, which for generations has labeled the town "the jewel." Day after day for many an hour I walked this pathway with my New Testament. Sometimes I sat to pray or stood in silence to commune, or simply waited in prayerful mood. And the living Lord met me. There was no doubting His identity. He broke in upon me with startling clarity. Sometimes it was in correction or judgment. Sometimes He came with a new insight or fresh discovery of truth. At particular places He drew me with extraordinary vividness. So real was the living Christ at some places on that walk that to have been with any other would have been sacrilege.

For you that familiar place of encounter may be a room in your home, a tiny chapel, a wayside shrine or a church. Wherever it is, He will meet us with the old salutation "Peace be with you!" And you will not mistake Him.

Another lesson we learn from the two first after-Easter Sundays is that He comes to each of us in our own experience. Although He was vivid to all of them, each individual had his own encounter, his personal authentication, his sense of reality, and the personal certification of His face. The disciples were so sure of the living Christ, so overwhelmed by the reality, that they made no effort to analyze "how" He came into that room or the kind of body with which He came. The miracle of His being there, the indubitable identity of the Presence, the reality of the Person of the resurrected Christ attested all lesser miracles of method and substance. He stood before the disciples in some miraculous way. And although He spoke to them, He did not discourse on the miracle. He cemented the reality.

Maybe the living Christ will come to you as He came to the renowned R. W. Dale of Carr's Lane Church, Birmingham, England. For many years Dr. Dale had been a follower of Christ, an able scholar and effective preacher. Then one day with books and papers spread upon his desk and table, as he worked on an Easter sermon, the reality of the presence of the Resurrected One swept over him, filled his consciousness and so elevated his insight that he began to pace up and down the floor shouting, "Jesus Christ is alive! Jesus Christ is alive!" What had been before a glib fact and conventional practice, in that moment became a glowing reality. Every Sunday thereafter an Easter hymn was sung in Carr's Lane Church. Every day became resurrection day to Dr. Dale. More beautiful than in art, profounder than in theology, clearer than any historic fact can be, the living Christ Himself came into Dr. Dale's personal experience.

"He comes to us as One unknown," wrote Albert Schweitzer, "without a name, as of old by the lake-side He came to those who knew Him not. He speaks to us the same word, 'Follow thou Me,' and sets us to the task which He has to fulfil for our time. He commands. And to those who obey Him, whether they be wise or simple, He will reveal Himself in the toils, the conflicts, the sufferings which they shall pass through in His fellowship,

41

and, as an ineffable mystery, they shall learn in their own experience who He is."

The word heard on those after-Easter Sundays was the common salutation, "Peace be with you!" But to them, as it must be to us, it is not the peace of escape or quietude but the peace of forgiveness, of hope, of new life, of perennial power. When we open our consciousness and He comes in we say from hearts welling up with joy and overflowing with reality, "My Lord and my God!"

3 The Word of Faith

> *"Blessed are they that have not seen, and yet have believed." (John 20:29)*

THOMAS SOUGHT AND received a personal certification of his faith. The risen Lord did not regard him as more obdurate or sinful than the other disciples. Thomas appeared on the second Sunday evening as an honest man seeking personal validation of an event reported by others but which he could not accept on their findings alone. To Thomas it was too important a matter to be satisfied so easily. If this were all true, it was so tremendous, Thomas thought, that it must have unimpeachable evidence.

The risen Christ of the Upper Room revealed only tenderness and understanding. Thomas was troubled and the Lord wanted him to have assurance. He wanted Thomas to be certain that He who now had fellowship with the disciples was identical with the Person they had seen crucified on Friday. Every condition Thomas required was fulfilled. But Thomas seems not to have explored with his fingers the resurrected body standing before him that night. The identifying cicatrix, though not fingered, must have been apprehended in some other way. Thomas was sure. Christ was so vivid, so real, so overwhelming in the majesty of His personality that Thomas called Him by name, shouting in ecstasy and adoration. Then the resurrected Christ left with Thomas a word to hearten every follower of the Master in all generations: "Thomas," said Jesus, "have you believed because you have seen me? Blessed are those who have not seen and yet believe." [1] Here the living Christ set down the eternal principle that the Christian life is a walk of faith supported by something higher and surer than the experience of a single sense.

The Scriptures teach us that Jesus did many signs in the presence of the disciples which are not written; but the record which we have is written that men may believe that Jesus is the Christ, the Son of the living God. After the resurrection Jesus taught His disciples that the Christian life is a life of faith. He came to the disciples in their temples and in their tasks as though He were teaching them that there would be no experience into which He would not enter.

That is the meaning of the episode related in the

44

Twenty-first Chapter of St. John. A half dozen or so of
the disciples had gone fishing. They had toiled through
the long night hours and were headed with an empty
boat for the shore. On the beach they caught the glim-
mer of a fire and beside it stood a man. Across the lake
that person called out, "Children, have ye any meat?" To
which they made dejected reply, "No!" "Then cast the
net on the right side." [2] The fishermen promptly heeded
the advice and when they put pressure on the nets they
discovered that the nets were so laden with fish they
could hardly be tugged ashore. When at last they had
reached the beach they found the Master, and with Him
cooked a meal over the coals of the fire and consumed
it together. In an immediate awareness of the Person on
the shore they exclaimed, "It is the Lord."

The narrative follows with these words, "Now none of
the disciples dared ask him, 'Who are you?' They knew
it was the Lord." [3] He came to them a Person to persons.
They simply *knew* the Lord. And so for forty days and
forty nights He came to the disciples—to individuals, to
couples, to small groups, to a crowd of five hundred, in
at least ten or eleven appearances. It was clear that there
was to be no place or activity into which He might not
come. He might come to them in the synagogue, in the
Upper Room, while they worked at the bench, or in the
fields, or fishing. The communication was between persons. The Person of the living Christ communicated

45

with the persons who were His disciples. It was always Person to person encounter. Jesus Christ risen from the dead became vivid and real in their consciousness, as real in His personality as the Person with whom they had walked the Galilean highways for three years and whom they had seen crucified—as real as any other person among them anywhere at any time. Then, after establishing His abiding presence in their consciousness, He went out of the sight of these men in order to be near to all men.

What Jesus became in the days following His resurrection, He is forever. What He was to the disciples He is to be to each of us—and in the same manner. Blessed are those who have not seen and yet believe.

How is it that He comes to us if indeed He comes to us as He came to them? This was personality meeting personality. What is personality? Nobody has really given us a satisfactory definition. Personality is mysterious and illusive. We can meet and know and have experiences with a person, but we have difficulty defining personality.

We know what personality is not. It is not a mere physical animal of flesh and bone and blood, of glands, with a nervous system, a respiratory system and a circulatory system. Personality is more than a material substance compounded of salt, lime, potash, and phosphorous, although the human body contains these chemicals and many more. That chemical compound, that material substance, changes, we are told, every seven years. It cannot be that we are known to each other in this limited way. Although the body is the home of the spirit for our earthly life and the instrument through which personality is revealed, persons are more than that.

Personality is something deep, hidden, indefinable, but vivid and real to other persons. Personality is a composite of mind, emotion, will and body, characterized by a distinct type of temperament. Personality is that which makes us identifiable as individuals, makes you what you are and me what I am. Personality is that distinctive essence which is the sum total of being, and which makes each of us an unduplicated entity among the millions of persons in all the universe. We know people; we get across to people; and they get through to us by some hidden quality—a mysterious reciprocity of spirit, an attitude of life, a warmth of being. Mind gets through to mind, heart to heart, soul to soul, character to character. Persons are identifiable to other persons in terms beyond physical and material substance.

So the resurrection of Christ was the coming again in power of the same discernible, identifiable, communicating, indubitable Person—the Person of Jesus whom they had known before, now risen in the majesty of His resurrected personality. This reality is sufficient for faith.

It is the heart of the gospel news. It attests the truth that the resurrection of Jesus was a real resurrection and that the living Christ can be to us today what He was on the first Easter.

If the living Christ came as a Person to persons in their own experience, we then ask how it is that any person becomes a reality in personal experience. This is an age-old question. What is the nature of reality? The philosophers and metaphysicians have not yet made up their minds as to whether reality is wholly objective or subjective. Is some person real only because there is a material substance at a given spot which can be measured and certified? Except there be other eyes to perceive and minds to interpret, how can you "know" there is another at that place? Or do we know a person by a total experience both within us and without us? Of this we may be certain: if someone exists outside us and we are aware of his existence, there is an image or picture on the mind which is in correspondence with the outward reality which is that person. This is the way you know me. This is the way I know you. If I exist and you know that I exist as a real being at this moment, there is on the screen of your mind an image or picture which corresponds to the man who is writing these words. In human experience this is the way of reality. Persons are known to other persons because there is an image or picture on the mind which is identical to the person who actually exists outside the observing person. This suggests that imagination is God's gift to us for faith. By the image on the inside in actual human experience we are made aware of the reality on the outside, which is the person we are comprehending.

This is one of the most glorious discoveries for Christian experience. The way of faith is reinforced by the instrumentality of personal experience as personality gets through to personality by God's gift of imagination.

The saints are the geniuses of the spirit. "Genius is childhood refound at will," wrote the late Cardinal Mercier, Belgium's World War I church hero. This is simply another way of saying what our Lord said long ago, "Except ye be converted; and become as little children, ye shall not enter into the kingdom. . . ." [4] What is the nature of childhood? It is to have a vivid imagination. Images come readily and brilliantly to the mind of a little child. The child is at home in two worlds, the seen and the unseen, the visible and the invisible. Looking out of the window while it is raining, the little child exclaims, "God is crying!" Or gazing into the cloud-filled sky, the little girl sees angels hanging out their laundry, or the boy sees Roy Rogers on a white horse. The night is filled with a thousand eyes. The dewdrops become myriad sparkling jewels.

> Will there really be a morning?
> Is there such a thing as day?
> Could I see it from the mountains
> If I were as tall as they?

Has it feet like water-lilies?
Has it feathers like a bird?
Does it come from famous countries
Of which I have never heard?

Oh, some scholar, Oh, some sailor,
Oh, some wise man from the skies,
Please to tell a little pilgrim
Where the place called morning lies? [5]

That is the nature of childhood—it is sensitive imagination eternally fascinated by both what is seen and what is unseen. In childhood the temporal and the eternal know no distinction.

So Jesus said we should become not little children with unmanageable appendages and unpredictable demeanor, but as little children with imagination and simple faith.

Jesus is God's supreme gift to imagination. He brings to us the fulness of God's Person and Being. The New Testament tries to make this clear. In his letter to the Colossians, Paul says that Christ is "the image of the invisible God." God is a spirit. God is invisible. No man has seen God but we may know God. We have Jesus. Thank God, He may become as real to us as any other person we have ever known. Because all persons come to us as images, there comes in our own vivid experience the image of the invisible God. The writer of the Hebrews refers to Jesus as "the brightness of his glory and the express image of his person." Jesus Christ is God's gift to man for experiencing His personal and eternal Presence. We say it reverently. Jesus Christ is God's gift to faith. No wonder the risen Christ then said, "Blessed are they that have not seen and yet have believed." The same experience which Thomas had in seeing Jesus may be the experience we may have of the risen Christ without "seeing" what Thomas actually saw.

The living Christ came as a Person to persons. He comes now as a Person to persons. On that first Easter dawn the risen Lord would not let Mary touch Him. He simply said, "Mary" and He came a living Person to a person in experience. So He came in the Upper Room, a living Presence in the experience of the disciples. So He was made known as He walked on the Emmaus highway. The image and the reality were one. The Person communicating with the disciples was the same Person with whom they had walked the highways before. So Jesus came then to individuals, to groups, and to congregations of people, teaching them to walk by faith rather than by sight.

Jesus Christ has kept His promise. Wherever persons are assembled in His name He comes to them. Faith produces the image of His presence and the image and the reality are one. He comes to us as we read these pages this very moment. The world will comprehend

Him only as we become increasingly sure of His presence and certain that He supports us as we walk His way.

Sometimes I go to a mass in a Roman Catholic Church. Perhaps you do the same from time to time, even though you do not understand the movement at the altar or the doctrines which explain and sustain the action. There is something solemn and mysterious about the service and the simple trust of the worshipers which is deeply moving. So long as my faith is unobstructed, free and direct, so long as my imagination is uninhibited by physical distractions, the sense of Christ's Presence is there. He is there for me not because I see a red lamp symbolizing the Presence, but because of direct and immediate awareness.

There comes a time in that liturgy when for me the Presence is no longer there; that is the point at which the priest begins to serve the host to the communicant. And the reason the Presence departs is clear to me. When I contemplate that the devout participant believes that the substance taken into his mouth is actually *the* body of Christ, I am left unsatisfied. That destroys reality for me. Imagine during the first forty days after Easter someone handing Peter, or John, or Andrew a little wafer and saying "This is the Saviour." They would have been offended and shocked. This would almost be sacrilege. For them the living Christ was so vivid and so real that this would have destroyed the holy vision. They were so aware of Christ that they expected Him everywhere, anytime. In the fulness of His living Presence He was to them in His resurrected glory all that He had been before and more. When imagination is stifled faith is crippled, but when imagination is free it becomes an instrument of faith whereby the living Lord becomes real.

You can find Him real in church, in any church. He is more real in church, among His own people, than in any other place. That was His promise. But He is not limited to the church where sacerdotal miracles take place. When faith is free and imagination uninhibited the living Presence can in His fulness be to us what Jesus Christ was to His first disciples. In your own church, in a chapel, at a wayside shrine, in your own room, on a leisurely walk, beside a stream, when you are in tune, when you have learned the lesson Christ taught Thomas, He comes out of the everywhere into personal experience. He may be to us today all that He has ever been to His disciples.

Some time ago Ernest Dowsett wrote a book in which he related the episode of a Scottish minister in a highland village making a call upon a couple whom he wished to induce to a deeper commitment. As the minister approached the house through the gate, he noticed the well-kept garden and the neat arrangements of the home. He knocked at the door and waited. When the lady appeared he removed his hat and asked in his simple manner, "Does Jesus live here?"

The lady was somewhat taken aback and there was an embarrassing silence, so he asked again, "Does Jesus live here?" This time the woman fled through the house to the rear, found her husband and pantingly exclaimed, "John, John, the minister is here and has asked a curious question. John, he asked, 'Does Jesus live here?' " "Well, well, Mary," said her husband, "did you not tell him that on the Lord's day we go to the Kirk, and when we go to the Kirk we put our money in the plate? Did you not tell him that, Mary?"

"Aye, aye," said Mary, "that I was minded to do, John, but the minister asked, 'Does Jesus live here?' And that's different, John, that's different."

And it is different!

We have our stately churches, our exquisite chapels, our moving liturgies, our precisely phrased creeds, our efficient ecclesiastical systems. But there is a deeper, more searing question. Men and women and boys and girls want to know if we have the living Christ in our lives, in our homes, in our churches. Thank God, we may. For He is here; He is here now, the same today as He was yesterday and will be forever. What He was once He is eternally. He keeps His promise: "I will never leave thee nor forsake thee." [6] Across the ages comes His word, "Lo, I am with you always. . . ." [7] What He was to Thomas He may be to you and to all who open their lives to Him. "Blessed are they that have not seen, and yet have believed."

Christmas is for crusaders who will give their lives for a cause greater than merely knowing that Christ came to earth, but for going out where the sheep are and bringing them into His fold

4 The Word of Discipleship

"Do you love me? . . . Feed my sheep." (John 21:17, RSV)

THESE WORDS FROM the risen Saviour were spoken to Peter. On the afternoon of the first Easter Day, when Peter was alone in his own room and in deep despair, the resurrected Lord had appeared to Peter.[1]

After having had breakfast with the fishermen-disciples on the beach of Tiberius, the living Christ turned and engaged Peter in a dialogue. Peter, the disciple who first testified that Jesus was the Christ, the Son of the living God; Peter, whom the Master had called the rock; Peter, who three times in crises had denied his Lord, now hears Christ ask three times, "Do you love me?" And Peter hears the Lord's commission to service in the Kingdom.

57

"Do you love me more than these?" Christ inquired. Once the Master had honored him, naming him first in the apostolic band, always taking with Him into the most intimate affairs Peter, James, and John. Whenever these three were mentioned, Peter always was named first. One day Peter had been called from his fishing. He recognized the authority, the command spirit, the force of the personality of the Master. When Jesus said, "Follow me!" he abandoned his fishing. He did follow Jesus. He followed Him up and down the land in comfort and in hardship, over mountain and desert. He followed Him listening to His words, working for and expecting the Kingdom. He did a lot of rash and unpredictable things, yet somehow until nearly the end the presence of the Master had tempered him and steadied him for service. There were twelve disciples, but Peter was always named first.

Then one day, when Jesus' enemies had closed in on Him, Peter denied his association with Him. He made the denial to a little servant girl in the outer court of a ruler's palace. Jesus died, and Peter was ashamed of himself. Now that Christ was risen and Peter had recovered this awareness and the old strength was coming back to him, Christ asks, "Do you love me? Do you *now* love me? Do you love me *more* than these—do?" It was as though Jesus suggested, "Peter, you loved me and then denied me—you are always in danger of deserting. I am *now* here to ask you, Do you love me *now?* Do you love me more than these love me? Do you love me more than you love all else?"

Peter was sure that he loved Christ in spite of failure, disappointment and disloyalty. To Christ he says, "You know—you know, Lord, that I love you." Three times the risen Christ puts the question. Three times Peter replies, "*You know*, Lord" and the third time Peter adds, "You know everything, you know that I love you." The persistence of the resurrected Saviour persuades Peter that the living Christ is now Saviour and Judge. He is teaching Peter a lesson which will abide with him. The essence of discipleship is *love;* the response of that love is service.

The living Christ makes the lesson very clear. The proof of love for the Lord is service in His Kingdom. Did not Jesus teach the supreme worth of man? The incarnation attests the value of a human soul—God came in a Man. The atonement confirms the value of a human soul—the God-man died to redeem sinners. The teachings of the Master attest the value of a human soul. Think of His words about little children, of His attitude toward women, toward slaves, toward soldiers, merchants, tax collectors. Love is reflected in service to men. The soul of man is of supreme worth. The result of love, so the living Christ confirms, is outgoing service.

When a man like Peter is forgiven and restored to a position where he loves Christ "more than these"—and more than he loves anyone or anything else—and when grace is at work, service to Christ is inevitable. When a man has experienced the miracle of forgiveness, his dominant impulse is to serve God.

A man whose soul is filled to overflowing with gratitude does more of his own free will than is demanded of him, said Martin Luther. He would like to do the impossible and yet—this is true of all that a man does from this impulse of gratitude—he never reflects on what he does, he never dreams that he is doing anything out of the ordinary. His actions are free from all self-consciousness. "Faith does not ask whether it ought to do good works; it has done them already."

Notice the sequence of commissioning by which the living Christ emphasizes that service is prompted by love.

Jesus said, "Do you love me more than these?"

Peter replied, "Yes, Lord, you know that I love you."

Then Jesus said, "Feed my lambs."

The dialogue continued.

Jesus asked, "Simon, son of John, do you love me?"

Peter replied, "Yes, Lord; you *know* that I love you."

Jesus continued, "Tend my sheep."

A third time the truth is emphasized.

Jesus asked, "Simon, son of John, do you love me?"

Peter was now hurt by this persistent inquiry and answered, "Lord, you know everything; you know that I love you."

Jesus said again, "*Feed* my sheep."

It is made clear—made clear by our Lord's repetition —that if you love Him you will serve Him in a ministry to others. He is the Overshepherd. His apostles, His ministers are the undershepherds and they are to lead a people who are themselves outgoing in love and service.

The church is not truly Christ's church until it loses its life in a ministry to the world. A Christian is not fully a Christian until he is giving himself, his testimony and his service to others. The church which is everlastingly fussing about itself, its prestige, its influence, its position, is hardly the true fellowship of Christ. The church which is self-centered and ingrown, pampering itself, fondling its own achievements, admiring its own righteousness, caressing its own virtues, while failing in evangelism and missionary zeal, is progressively denying its Lord. Whenever church members become excessively obsessed with their own privileges or their own comforts, or exclusively absorbed with their own spiritual state, to the neglect of an outgoing love, they are something less than Christ intended. Constantly feeling one's spiritual pulse, unduly assessing one's spiritual state, nervously looking on the inside, trying to keep for oneself the spiritual verities as a personal treasure, can make Christians chronic invalids of the spirit. The only way to grow in grace, to keep the spiritual glow, is to give it away. The Christian personality is not a reservoir where the water of life is stored but the spring where the water of life arises and flows out to others. If you love Christ you give yourself—you become a channel of spiritual grace. Love reaches out to others, to gather in the sheep and tend the flock of God.

There is a special message here for the ministers of Christ's church. With the passing of time, the qualifications for a minister of the church have become more and more clear. The first requisite is a love of Jesus Christ as Redeemer and Lord. However, the most important question to be answered by a candidate for the ministry is this: "Do you love people—all kinds of people? Can you know all there is to know about people, their strength and weakness, virtues and vices, their saintliness and sinfulness, and still keep on loving them? Can you know all there is to know about people and keep on loving them and believing in their redeemability?" Unless he has this attitude, he is not called to the ministry. To know when it is possible to help someone and to know when it is not possible to help someone, and to leave such persons in the tender care of Christ, the Overshepherd, is a mark of a mature minister of Christ. To know when to be tender and to know that at times the most therapeutic and the most Christlike ministry is to be firm and forceful—that too is the mark of the minister of Christ.

There were three commissions given by the risen Christ to Peter. When Peter said he loved Christ, our Lord first said, "Feed my *lambs*." Some there are in the flock who are innocent and ignorant, helpless and tender, immature and ungrown. "Feed my *lambs.*" There are persons newly born into the Kingdom who need to learn the elemental truths of the gospel. This is a lesson we need to learn in our present religious revival. Hosts of Americans are just over the doorstep into the church. They have "confessed" Christ, but their comprehension is small indeed. They require patient teaching, cultivation, fellowship and love if they are to be mature. The lambs must be born into the fold but they need a lamb's food and a lamb's care until they develop a sheep's strength and a sheep's appetite.

Then the living Christ said to Peter that if he loved Him he should *tend* the sheep. "*Tend* my sheep." The sheep belong to Christ's fold. They are not the undershepherd's or sheeptender's flock but the flock of God and the Overshepherd directs the undershepherd to "tend the sheep." The sheep are not all the same in their personal characteristics and needs.

This speaks right to the modern church. Once the church was almost the only place where the members assembled. Once a pastor could begin at the end of a street and systematically call in every home of the congregation. In a year or two, in a small or an average church, the shepherd got around to each of the members of the flock. But today, although the minister may spend and be spent in devotion to duty, such cannot be done by a single individual. So the church becomes a fellowship of small, intimate groups within the whole church. There is an authentic ministry in more than one pastor in a church and in a division of pastoral labor. In order to express our love of Christ and *tend* the flock of God and do it better, we have a multiple ministry. In order to serve individual persons more faithfully and more efficiently, there are several ministers and many lay helpers. This makes the large institutional church more personal in its solicitude, its concern and pastoral care. And this makes the church more like the primitive church.

The third commission given by the risen Christ to Peter is *"Feed* my sheep." The first was *"Feed* the lambs"—the newly born, the children, the infants in faith, the immature. The second direction was to *"tend"* the entire flock of varied peoples with diverse needs. And lastly Christ says, *"Feed* my sheep." They are His sheep who are to be fed. And with what are they to be fed? They are truly the sheep of Christ's fold and remain such when they are fed the Word of God, the truths of the Scriptures, the gospel of redeeming grace. People have had enough of amateur politicians, synthetic sociologists, and tyro economists in the pulpit. Men's souls crave the word from God. They want certitude and assurance, the meat of the gospel. They need the nourishment which comes from prayer and praise and instruction. They do not want ambiguity or uncertainty about the gospel. Instinctively man is strengthened when he hears the prophet of God say, "Thus saith the Lord." They need content and substance, the pure word of God, effectively presented in love. Nothing is so desperately needed today as that Christians shall really comprehend the gospel, the meaning and message of the church, and the requirements of Christian discipline. *"Feed* my sheep"—all of them—the firm and the fickle, the immature and mature, the failures and the successes. *"Feed* my sheep."* That is the role of Peter and all in apostolic succession. At least one of the marks of apostolic succession is love of the faithful. Another is the act of feeding them the food Christ has provided for His people.

The first and the last lesson of Christianity is love. "Thou shalt love the Lord thy God." "A new commandment give I unto you, That ye love. . . . By this shall all men know that ye are my disciples, if ye have love. . . ." [2] Authentic apostolic succession is vested in those who love Christ and "feed" the faithful. Over and over again the living Christ asks, "Do you love me?" And to all who make Peter's reply, the eternal Lord of the church commands, "Feed my sheep!"

5 The Word for the World

> *"And Jesus came and said to them, 'All au-*
> *thority in heaven and on earth has been given*
> *to me. Go therefore and make disciples of all*
> *nations, baptizing them in the name of the*
> *Father and of the Son and of the Holy Spirit,*
> *teaching them to observe all that I have com-*
> *manded you; and lo, I am with you always, to*
> *the close of the age.'"* (Matthew 28:18–20,
> RSV)

THE FIRST BOOK in the New Testament has been called
the Gospel of the Three Mountains. In the Gospel according to Matthew each mountain is an altitude in the
ministry of our Lord. The Mountain of the Beautitudes
sets forth the basic principles in His ministry. The Mountain of the Transfiguration was a culminating moment
of spiritual exultation. The Mountain of the Great
Commission stands at the end of His ministry and the
launching of the world-wide conquest of the gospel. It

is with this episode that the Gospel of Matthew closes, and in which we find the words, "And Jesus came and said to them, 'All authority in heaven and on earth has been given to me. Go therefore and make disciples of all nations, baptizing them in the name of the Father and of the Son and of the Holy Spirit, teaching them to observe all that I have commanded you; and lo, I am with you always, to the close of the age.' "

Jesus loved the mountains. To the mountains He went to pray. It was after praying all night upon a mountain that He chose twelve men to be His apostles. On the mountain, in the presence of the inner circle, He was transfigured. On the mountain He met and rejected the tempter. On the mountain He won His first great victory. On a mountain in Galilee He would make His last great declaration. On a mountain the first-generation Christians received their marching orders. On a mountain the church was given its foreign policy.

John Ruskin calls the mountains "these great cathedrals of the earth, with their gates of rock, pavements of cloud, choirs of stream and stone, altars of snow, and vaults of purple traversed by the continual stars, full of treasures of illuminated manuscript for the scholar, kindly in simple lessons to the worker, quiet in pale cloisters for the thinker, glorious in holiness for the worshiper."

It was to a cathedral in the sky that the disciples were summoned where in the pure air they might feel the presence of the Holy God, and face to face receive from the risen Christ His last words of comfort and command.

Once on a mountain the tempter had proposed: "All these things [the kingdoms of the world, and the glory of them] will I give to thee, if thou wilt fall down and worship me." [1] Jesus scorned the offer but went on to the bitter end to win the world by sacrifice and love. No bribe to short-cut the way to glory could turn Him from the requirements of His redemptive mission. What He would not take from the Evil One He will gain by the power of the gospel message.

On the day appointed, the followers of Jesus converged on the mountain. They came from distant villages, from Capernaum and Bethsaida and elsewhere. Alone and in groups they made their way through the many valleys to the designated mountain, where they found the apostles and the Jerusalem followers and confirmed the word that this was surely the time and place for the meeting. Thus, it appears, that several hundred of Jesus' followers gathered on some elevated fastness near the sea of Galilee. The Jerusalem meeting had been in a closed room at night. This meeting was in broad daylight in the out-of-doors. Perhaps the disciples stood apart on a promontory. All waited in awe and expectant mood.

Then before the entire assembly the Radiant One appeared. This was the third time since the resurrection that He had appeared to a large company. In a vast surge of emotion the whole company was swept by a common irresistible impulse to worship the living Christ; they fell on their knees in adoration of the exalted, victorious Lord.[2]

All the past was preparation. The time for realizing the coming Kingdom had arrived. Here at the confluence of the ages stood the central figure of all history, the resurrected Christ, the Incarnate God.

Now listen to His words, spoken to fishermen and humble folk. Theirs is to be the greatest work of which man has ever heard or thought. The first missionaries of Jesus were commanded to "Go not into the way of the Gentiles, and into any city of the Samaritans enter ye not; But go rather to the lost sheep of the house of Israel." [3] But now these people are given a broader task. The prophet of Israel has become the Christ of the Nations and the Redeemer of Men. The limitations of the first commission are removed. His influence now will be limitless. His domain will be the whole world. He now inaugurates a campaign not for the years but for eternity, not for Palestine but for the whole world. No lips ever uttered such words before. No human being ever asserted such unlimited authority.

He speaks with authority and power. Every disciple is now to be a commissioned officer in a militant church. They are to be educated in the mind of Christ and in conduct worthy of the Master. They are to be trained until they have mastered not simply a creed but a character. They are to observe all the Saviour has taught them.

Here on the Mountain of Commissioning every Christian is made a missionary. He is to go in person or by substitute to represent Christ. There is no escaping it. This is His first and authentic command.

Once a group of Christians, in the presence of the Duke of·Wellington, was discussing the wisdom of prosecuting foreign missions when the Duke turned upon them with a sharp rejoinder, "Look to your marching orders!" Here on the mountain in Galilee Christians received their marching orders. The church is to be a missionary church. Its message is a message for the whole world. And its conquests one of the marvels of history.

"The power is mine," He was saying. "The people are mine," He claimed. "Go in the power I give—I will be with you."

Jesus claimed authority to speak in the Father's name. He claimed authority to forgive sins; he claimed authority over evil spirits. He claimed authority to give eternal life to all whom the Father had given Him. Now He claims authority transcending all others. He claims *universal* authority. The whole creation—heaven and earth —are his. The resurrection gave Him this final, supreme authority. He was "declared to be the Son of God with power . . . by the resurrection from the dead." [4]

First He said, "All authority . . . has been given to me." Then He said, "I am with you always." The first is an assertion of unlimited power. The last is the promise of an omnipotent Presence.

There is no such thing as a Christian church which is not missionary in spirit and purpose. Any other attitude is a distortion of the commission and disobedience to the clear command of the risen Christ. The sequence is clear: 1. Unlimited power; 2. Go; 3. Teach; 4. Baptize (evangelize); 5. The living Presence forever.

The great commission gave the church its foreign policy. For centuries the Christian message was carried only by direct evangelism and its success was measured in terms of individual converts. While continuing aggressively with direct personal evangelism, we now know there are other ways of witnessing and winning for Christ.

Direct evangelism is the first method for winning the world. But the foreign policy of the church may be said to be effective when there is the penetration of a culture with Christian ideals and ethics. Take, for example, what has happened in the Middle East. Students of world religions know that a Moslem is rarely converted to Christianity by outright enrollment; when this happens he is completely disinherited by his family, his community, his society. Yet the Christian cause has made a tremendous impact on the lands in which both Islam and Christianity arose.

More than a hundred years ago, little schools began to be established in Beirut, Cairo, Bagdad, Damascus,

72

Aleppo, Tehran and elsewhere. They were to educate people—all kinds of people, of many races and nations. Those who did the educating were, for the most part, Christians. They were simply living a Christian life, letting other people know what a Christian is like, and letting it be known that this was the love of Christ in action. They were not aggressively seeking converts; they merely loved people and taught them. And what has happened? These colleges and universities have been the greatest single ameliorating influence in the whole Middle East. When the United Nations was organized at the Convention in San Francisco, there were more graduates from the American University of Beirut on the delegations than from any other educational institution in the world. And that University is the direct result of the missionary imperative. More important than this has been the gradual change in the attitudes of the people toward public service, toward human welfare, toward the status of women and the institution of marriage and the home. Through Christian motivated education, cultural changes take place and the Kingdom of Christ is extended.

Take the ministry of healing. The Communion table in The National Presbyterian Church in Washington is made of wood from the Cedars of Lebanon. How did that happen? Late in the last century a group of women of the congregation of this church sent the first woman physician to the Middle East. Dr. Mary Eddy, with one nurse and a dozen beds in an old shed, started a hospital. That hospital is now the largest and best tubercular sanitarium in eight surrounding nations. And it is named for one of my predecessors, Dr. Tunis Hamlin. Hamlin Memorial Hospital is the outgrowth of the Christian missionary impulse of an historic American church. The wood for the table was an expression of appreciation for this gift of love. Without counting converts, only by showing the love of Christ, whole cultures have been penetrated and transformed.

It is possible also to carry out the missionary imperative by direct acts of friendship. In our church in Washington, situated as it is only a few blocks from the White House and in the heart of the embassies, we have ample opportunity to demonstrate the friendship of the Christian American. Not only do we welcome our foreign guests to church services but we literally "bring them in." Such occasions are the series of International Friendship Dinners held annually in the Church Hall. On one recent occasion we were hosts to people from fifty-two nations representing five races. They appeared in native dress. Many gave their greetings first in their own language and then in ours. The whole program was recorded by the Voice of America. We had nothing to "sell" except friendship and love. There could be no concealment of this Christian hospitality. It was a Christian act and a Christian program through and through. The impressions of America and of Christians in America would be derived from such experiences as these. We ought neither to parade nor conceal our Christian witness. When we are most truly ourselves we are a friendly, warmhearted, outgoing, spiritual people. We ought to let Christ work through us in friendly ways.

Another outreach of the Christian cause today is through the representatives of our nation in foreign lands, through our governmental representatives and all others who live, work or travel abroad. There ought never to be any "Ugly Americans"—any unworthy Americans roaming the earth. We ought not to tolerate such models at home. An American is most truly an American and a representative of our culture, our freedom, and our institutions when he is most thoroughly Christian. Moreover, it is our spiritual character and our sincere religious practice which gets through most quickly to influence other people, more than any other single act or fact. American diplomats, for instance, often accomplish more by going to church and maintaining their religious devotions than by many of the official routine acts they are called upon to perform. There should be no concealment of the personal Christian witness. We are respected when we are respectable. Other peoples are spiritually sensitive and spiritually hungry and other peoples will understand us better in these terms than in terms of our material and scientific achievement. This emphasizes the need for Christians to enter the diplomatic service as a Christian vocation, a way of life honored by God and in service to God under the nation's auspices, for the welfare of all mankind.

So the Commission given on the mountain that day is still before us. Nothing given by Christ has ever been taken away. A command—to go. An order—to teach. A formula of initiative—to baptize. Above all else—power to witness and to serve—and the blessed assurance of His presence forever.

He bids us keep everlastingly at work until:

> . . . every kindred, every tribe,
> On this terrestrial ball,
> To Him all majesty ascribe
> And crown Him Lord of all.[5]

6 The Word from the Living Word

"Did not our hearts burn within us while he talked to us on the road, while he opened to us the scriptures?" (Luke 24:32, RSV)

ONE OF THE most felicitous stories in all literature is that of the two disciples on their way to Emmaus. It carries with it the deepest inward evidence of its own truthfulness. There is a sense of utter reality about it. It is one of the most beautiful stories in the most beautiful books ever written.

Late on the first Easter Sunday afternoon, two disciples of Jesus are walking together over the road from Jerusalem to Emmaus, which is a distance of seven or eight miles. It was a hot afternoon and they walked with slow pace, characteristic of people on the desert. Quite likely they stopped when their conversation became intensely interesting, and this delayed their journey. While deeply engaged in conversation, another person joins them. They did not notice the third person, who must also have been coming from Jerusalem, but when He asked them what they were talking about so earnestly, they stopped short in their surprise and made answer.

One of the disciples named Cleophas answered, "Are you the only visitor to Jerusalem who does not know the things that have happened there in these days?" [1] The disciples were sad in countenance and disconsolate in spirit. The stranger asked, "What things?" And they replied, "Concerning Jesus of Nazareth, who was a prophet mighty in deed and word before God and all the people, and how our chief priests and rulers delivered him up to be condemned to death, and crucified him. But we had hoped that he was the one to redeem Israel. Yes, and besides all this, it is now the third day since this happened." [2]

There was a sob in his heart and a lament in his spirit as Cleophas stopped and tried to say that all of the disciples had hoped that He might have redeemed Israel but that even this mighty prophet, like other prophets, had been put to death.

But there was a later report which Cleophas mentioned: "Some women of our company amazed us. They were at the tomb early in the morning and did not find

78

his body; and they came back saying that they had even seen a vision of angels, who said that he was alive. Some of those who were with us went to the tomb, and found it just as the women had said; but him they did not see." [3]

At this point the stranger interjected a rebuke: "O foolish men, and slow of heart to believe all that the prophets have spoken!" [4] "Why are you so slow to believe?" He seemed to ask. "Why be in such needless sorrow? Why not open your mind and heart to the truth of the Scriptures? If you had more understanding you would have more faith. Your despondency arises out of your inability to see the meaning of the Scriptures." It requires spiritual perception to read the word of God aright. It takes strength of intellect and clarity of understanding to achieve a sturdy and immovable faith.

Then the stranger began an exposition of Moses and all the prophets, interpreting to them the meaning of the Scriptures. The lesson had such a ring of authority about it, and the truths became so self-evident, that their despair began to disappear and a new hope blazed in their hearts as they listened.

As they approached the village the sun was aglow in the west over the Mediterranean and darkness would soon settle over the land. As they drew near the door of the Emmaus home, the stranger was about to say farewell and go down the road toward the Mediterranean to Lydda or Joppa when they asked Him to stay for supper:

"Stay with us, for it is toward evening and the day is far spent." [5] When the meal was prepared, because He was a rabbi who had much knowledge of the Scripture and was a master of the law, they put Him at the head of the table. He blessed the bread, broke it and gave it to them. They had never known anyone except Jesus to expound the Scriptures with such force and meaning. As He gave them the bread and they reflected on the highway conversation, they were amazed to discover that this was Jesus, their own Master, Jesus of Nazareth, who had been crucified and buried—Jesus, the risen Lord, sitting at their own table giving them bread. Then as their vision became clearer and they recognized Him, He vanished out of their sight. In this moment of realization they gasped, looking at each other saying, "Did not our hearts burn within us while he talked to us on the road, while he opened to us the scriptures?" So overwhelming was this experience with the living Christ that they immediately arose from the table and dashed over the road back to Jerusalem to find the other disciples and report the good news. With burning hearts, in the thrill of an awareness of Jesus, they went back to the scene of Friday's defeat and announced to their friends that the Lord had risen, had walked with them, had taught them the Scriptures, had eaten with them and even while they ate, had suddenly vanished. What they had heard as a report from other disciples they had now corroborated in their own personal experience.

In the preceding chapter our text has been a quotation from the risen Christ. Now we think of Christ, the living Word, the One who validates all spoken words. He is the Word which makes all other words, written or uttered, come to life. The Word which became flesh and dwelt among us, the Word which men beheld in life is now risen in the glory of a new life. The living Word makes all other words luminous and clear.

There were two reasons why the disciples reported that their hearts burned within them. Their hearts burned because they had suddenly become aware of the living Christ. Had He not brought to them something which no man had ever brought to this world before? He spoke as never man had spoken. They had watched Him preach and teach and heal. They had followed Him throughout the villages and the cities. He had brought a luster to life which could only have been conveyed to them by One whose identification was with eternal and elemental things. Somehow they believed Him to be more than a prophet. They had hoped He was the Messiah, for He met all the qualifications of the Redeemer of Israel.

Then He was put to death. When He died, their hopes died with Him. But not wholly! Faith had been diminished but faith had not wholly disappeared. Then, as they walked and talked and dined, the One whom they had loved walked back into their lives into their own personal experience. He talked with them. He walked with them. He ate with them. He entered into the same experiences with them in which they had found such blessed companionship before. In a moment of exultant awareness they knew, they simply *knew* that He was alive and real. What He had been once He became to them again on that journey: an unmistakable, communicating, vivid Person known to them in their own experience. The fire of faith was rekindled. They were so sure that Jesus survived death that they sprinted back to add their report to the accumulating reports from other disciples. No wonder their hearts burned within them. This was the incandescence of personal experience.

They were sure it was the living Christ not only by immediate awareness but by the authentic interpretation of the Scriptures. The man who walked on the highway first asked them some questions, and then as they traveled He opened to them the meaning of the Scriptures. They were steeped in Jewish tradition and familiar with the principal events of Jewish history. The companion talked about Moses and instructed them concerning the meaning of the prophets and then turned to a discussion of the events in the career of Jesus of Nazareth. As He talked, it dawned upon them that what had taken place in Jerusalem in recent days was the fulfillment of the Scriptures. The presence of the living Christ clarified history and brought meaning and understanding to recent events. The One whom the evangelists later called the living Word brought to these disciples in their personal experience an understanding of the written Word.

The living Christ and the Scriptures have ever been bound together. It is the Person of Jesus Christ who gives meaning to the Bible. It is the living Christ who brings light and understanding to the Bible. Apart from Jesus Christ, the Word of God is an enigma. When men "experience Christ," the Bible becomes intelligible. It is a fact of Christian history that when men are converted to Jesus Christ the Scriptures begin to have a meaning which they did not have before. Whenever men come to God by Jesus Christ, asking God's forgiveness, whenever they cast themselves on God's mercy and redeeming love made known in Christ, whenever by personal faith they accept the redemption freely offered through Christ, there comes to them not only an overwhelming sense of love and joy and thanksgiving for what Christ has done, but there comes a craving for the Word of God. The result of personal faith in Christ is an eagerness to know the Scriptures. It is the living Christ in personal life that unlocks the door to the Scriptures. The Person and the Book are inseparable. The whole Bible is the portrayal of God's action on man's behalf which is brought to fulfillment in the life, the atoning death and the resurrection of Jesus Christ from the dead. Men come into an immediate, direct experience with the living Christ and the Scriptures become alive. The truths of the New Testament were already concealed in the Old Testament. The truths of the Old Testament, through an experience with Christ, are revealed in the New Testament.

What depth of meaning, what riches of fellowship, what exaltation of the spirit comes when the living Christ and the holy Scriptures are joined together!

Walking in deep despair that day, the two disciples had a resurrection experience. The only Scriptures they had known, up to then, were the Old Testament Scriptures; now the Person of the New Testament revealed to them the meaning of the Old Testament. Hope was reborn, faith was kindled, new life dawned upon them and the whole world came to regard these two disciples as the apostles of the glowing heart. So it has ever been. The living Christ walking into our personal experience throws light and meaning upon history and upon the pages of the Word of God.

There is a lesson here we Christians must never forget. On the first Easter, when Sunday became the Sabbath for Christians, the risen Christ spent several hours with these disciples and their Bibles. The greatest of all Biblical expositors gave these two humble disciples instruction, interpretation, and exposition of the Scriptures. What a truth for us in our day! Nothing is more needed than that we shall find in our churches, Sunday after Sunday, the Word of God taught and proclaimed and interpreted in and by the spirit of the living Christ. And when it comes to preaching, is there anything that so satisfies the longing of men's souls and the need for spiritual nourishment as the Word of God spoken and interpreted by men whose minds have been kindled by an experience with the living Christ? It is the Incarnate Word, alive forevermore in the church, who gives light and life to the written Word.

Once on a highway long ago hearts were made to glow as the living Christ opened the Scriptures. They are never really opened until we know Him. That same Presence is with us today to make the Word of God a lamp unto our feet and a light to our pathway, and a highway to the living God.

> Will not our hearts within us burn
>   On the darkening road,
> If a White Presence we can discern—
>   Despite an ancient load?
>
> Whither goest Thou, Pilgrim Friend?
>   Lone Figure far ahead,
> Wilt Thou not tarry until the end—
>   And break our bread?
>
> Follow we must amid sun or shade,
>   Our faith to complete,
> Journeying where no path is made—
>   Save by His feet! [6]

7 The Word That Converts

"I am Jesus, whom you are persecuting." (Acts 9:5, RSV)

AMONG ALL THE apostles, Paul was the one most like us. He had not seen Jesus in the flesh. Unlike the others who bore witness to the resurrection, he had no precrucifixion experience with Jesus. Yet he believed in the resurrection, he lived by its power and he was the most persistent preacher of the gospel of the resurrection in the New Testament. Next to the resurrection itself, the conversion of the proud Pharisee was the most important event in the history of the church.

Paul was the greatest intellect of his generation. He was keen of eye and keen of mind, merciless in logic and a lover of truth. He possessed superior legal talent. He knew the laws of scientific evidence. He hated hypocrisy, and he loathed a lie. He would not believe except on the most complete, authentic, and incontestable accumulation of evidence. He could be conquered by nothing but truth.

He was a zealot in his devotion to Judaism and instinctively hostile to any faith with higher pretentions. He was renowned as the most bitter foe of the new sect in all the Jewish world. He made it his task to sweep Christianity from the face of the earth. He was the living, active incarnation of the Old World hostility to Jesus and His followers.

Yet Paul came to believe in the resurrection and to make it the center of all his preaching.

Paul had met and cross-examined Peter and the other apostles. He had met and questioned many of the five hundred or more disciples who had borne witness to the Easter events. He had watched them all through several years, and he had detected no evidence of collusion and no manifestation of delusion or hallucination. He had seen their lives incandescent with the light of resurrection reality. Under the fire of persecution, they shone as they burned, and they sang as they bled. He saw many of them die, like Stephen, with faces radiant with hope and triumphant in faith to the end.

Within five years after the event, this man of disciplined mind and massive intellect was convinced of the truth of the resurrection. Peter at Pentecost and the other disciples at Jerusalem and Judea and Samaria gave oral testimony to the resurrection, but it was Paul who provided the first written testimony. Some of his epistles are the earliest New Testament books to be written. They went to the churches before the Gospels were collated or the Book of Acts set down. In the very first letter —to the Thessalonians—Paul reminds them that they were saved "to serve a living and true God, and to wait for his Son from heaven, whom he [God] raised from the dead." [1] The living Christ and the new life in Him became the theme of the New Testament.

Paul was a man who required facts. He was no cloistered mystic. His feet were firmly planted on the ground. And the facts he found were that Jesus, who had been crucified on Friday before many witnesses, made Himself known in His resurrected reality to many witnesses on Sunday and during the subsequent forty days. Jesus who had walked and talked, dined and worked with men, after dying on the cross, had made Himself vivid to the consciousness of hosts of people. John writes near the end of his Gospel: "Now Jesus did many other signs in the presence of the disciples, which are not written in this book; but these are written that you may believe that Jesus is the Christ, the Son of God, and that believing you may have life in his name." [2]

The evidence could not be explained away nor refuted. Moreover, the reporters had such a personal experience they were reinvigorated, regenerated men who were willing to die for the cause. "Christ is risen!" was the burden of their witness. For them the divine mediation was with a living Person identical with the Jesus they had known in the flesh.

Paul, the ardent hater and defamer of Christians, became, by the power of the resurrection reality, the deathless crusader for the Christ who saved him. What a transformation! It was a more radical change than the change in the disciples between Friday night and Easter Sunday morning.

The spirit had ever been pursuing Paul, like the Hound of Heaven in Francis Thompson's poem. Then, walking down the Damascus highway, he was overwhelmed by a sudden dazzling light. A voice spoke to him, "Saul, Saul, why persecutest thou me? . . . I am Jesus, whom thou persecutest; it is hard for thee to kick against the pricks." [3] We all know the rest of the story. He was led into the city where his encounter with the living Christ continued until at last he stood up in the synagogues and proclaimed the living Lord who made all things new. Thereafter one central truth held Paul's allegiance—that he might "know him [Christ], and the power of his resurrection." [4] To the Christians in Rome he said that Jesus was "declared to be the Son of God with power, . . . by the resurrection from the dead." [5]

Paul's personal experience with the living Christ was corroborated by all his factual investigation of historic events. Historic events and personal experience confirmed and sustained each other, grew in his consciousness, expanded in his comprehension of truth, made Paul the greatest evangelist, missionary, and theologian of all time and the author of much of the Christian Scriptures.

Someone will say that Paul's experience with Christ was all subjective, and for this reason he could not be a valid witness to the resurrection. But this is like saying that some facts of experience are true, and other facts of experience are untrue. It would be like someone saying that *some* experiences in history are in fact true, while *other* experiences in history are not true because in fact they have not happened to the person rejecting the facts. But the events of personal experience are true events. The facts of experience are true facts. And the fact with which we are dealing here is that Paul asserts that his encounter was with the same Person with whom the disciples had fellowship following Easter Sunday morning.

To Christians, this should not create difficulties to faith. If we set forth our faith in a supernatural God as a premise, all else falls in order. For there are facts and realities which belong to the natural order and others which we believe belong to the supernatural order. Set down as the premise God the Father and His revelation of Himself in the Person of Jesus Christ, and the resurrection becomes not only credible but the principal certitude of our faith.

There are facts which are historical and there are facts beyond history. Historical facts are not capable of mathematical demonstration. We cannot prove the resurrection of Jesus as we can prove that two and two make four. History does not operate that way. Events appear whether or not they are predictable or explainable. They are reportable by historians but they are not to be proved in the laboratory or by the scientific method. History does not cover the whole realm of the possible, the actual, the certain and the real. The experiences of men confirm the reality of the resurrection. We have all the evidence for it of which such a fact admits. The resurrection occurred in history but its explanation is beyond the province of history.

"History is confined to the natural order of life. The supernatural, the miraculous, God and immortality, are all beyond the province of history. The historian as such has nothing to say either for or against. If he does, he does it as a theologian, or a metaphysician; but not in his capacity as a historian. . . . That Jesus died is historical. That He was buried is historical. That the grave was empty is a question purely within the limits of the historical. That the Galileans believed that they had seen Him after He was risen, is, as a psychological experience, within the limits of the historical. But the objective reality of His resurrection: this transcends the sphere of history. It is a dogmatic judgment, a venture of faith. . . . That the disciples passed through a tremendous change is within the historic sphere. But the cause of it lies outside that sphere and refuses to be brought within the circle of scientific critical investigation. Here the mere historian is baffled." [6]

When the scholar traces the faith back behind the Gospels to the period of the underlying primitive documentary sources, and still farther back to the oral tradition, it is discovered that there is no heightening of the view of the resurrection with the passing of the years. The very highest view is the earliest view. Christians do not worship a human life, which by some metamorphosis of deification climbed up to be God. We worship a God who came down into humanity by an act of incarnation, which is an event of a different quality. The resurrection is also an event of such a quality and belongs to a higher order. It was the living Christ Himself who validated the event.

Paul knew who Jesus was because he met Him. Paul met the same Person the disciples met during the forty days after the first Easter. The believer, even now, meets the same Person in recurrent experiences. Thus it must be understood that the modern Christian is not entirely dependent upon historical research for his knowledge of Jesus. That may be true for Caesar or Alexander or Napoleon, but not for Jesus.

Paul met the Person, Jesus Christ, who identified Himself saying, "I am Jesus, whom you are persecuting." To every believer on his own Damascus highway, in his own terms, the living Christ makes Himself known. To one He may come with the same overwhelming intensity with which He came to Paul; to another He may come by gradual disclosures until the believer simply "knows." By immediate awareness, in the depths of their being, men come to know in their own experience who our Lord is.

History does not cover the whole of reality. There are facts in personal experience which occur in the stream of history and the persons in whom the experiences occur modify history, but they are not subject to the ordinary rules of historical analysis. We can be just as certain of these facts of personal experience as we are certain that two and two make four. "Men have been as sure of the resurrection of Jesus as they were of any other fact in their knowledge. Men have been as sure of their resurrection life in Jesus as they have been of their own existence. They have been willing to stake all they had upon their certainty of it, and upon that same certainty they have hung all their hopes of the life to come. Judged by its results, the resurrection may be said to be the most certain fact in history. Judged by personal experience it may be regarded as more certain than any fact of history ever can be." [7]

Christianity is intelligent and logical to all who believe, whatever its enigma may be to unbelievers. The reality of our religion is rooted in personal experience.

Paul had his personal encounter with the living Christ. The Person he met was the same Person the disciples met in the days following the resurrection. The experiences of countless Sauls in church through twenty centuries attest this truth.

Paul was an intellectual. Paul was a legalist. Paul was a fundamentalist Jew. It was the risen Christ in personal experience who convinced him. Paul the person met Christ a Person, and all life was reversed. He heard the word that converted his whole being. Through the cataclysmic personal experience at Damascus, an intolerant bigot went out to become the greatest herald of the resurrection news. The persecutor became the persecuted. The resurrection became the theme of his preaching, his writing, his working, his living, his dying.

His life was absorbed in proclaiming the good news about the mighty acts of God through Jesus Christ who had redeemed him from blindness and death to light and life.

In his greatest message he reveals what the resurrection meant to him. "If you confess with your lips that Jesus is Lord and believe in your heart that God raised him from the dead, you will be saved. For man believes with his heart and so is justified, and he confesses with his lips and so is saved." [8]

Hear him again saying, "I am crucified with Christ: nevertheless I live; yet not I, but Christ liveth in me: and the life which I now live in the flesh I live by the faith of the Son of God, who loved me, and gave himself for me." [9]

So he preached and lived the converted life. Life to

Paul was Christ, and it had become so by and through personal conversion. "For to me to live is Christ, and to die is gain," [10] he called out. With that attitude he could not be defeated.

It was the resurrection experience which made him Paul. "That I may know him, and the power of his resurrection, and the fellowship of his sufferings" was the supreme ambition of his life. And so it was, and the world has been changed and the course of history redirected by this apostle.

The transformed life which St. Paul had may be yours. Your Damascus road may be in your church, your room at home, a chapel, or a hillside. When He speaks to you, let Him in—let Him in.

8 The Word To Be Preached

> *"And with great power gave the apostles witness of the resurrection of the Lord Jesus: and great grace was upon them all." (Acts 4:33)*

> *"And if Christ be not risen, then is our preaching vain, and your faith is also vain. Yea, and we are found false witnesses of God; because we have testified of God that he raised up Christ." (I Corinthians 15:14, 15)*

THE RESURRECTION OF Jesus was the great theme of apostolic preaching. The disciples went out from Jerusalem into the world not to preach ethics nor philosophic speculations but to announce a fact of history, and to describe a reality in their own existence. The burden of their preaching was "Jesus and the Resurrection." The teachings of Jesus, the miracles attributed to Him, the atoning death upon the cross, all derived their final meaning and their permanent significance from the resurrection. The good news which the disciples went out to proclaim was "Christ Is Risen!" That was the first distinctively Christian message to the world.

This gospel was preached because the resurrected Lord appeared to His own disciples and convinced them of His identity. Authentic preaching in true apostolic succession proclaims the same gospel.

Nobody saw the resurrection itself. There is little more than speculation about the manner in which it took place. The disciples believed in the resurrection because the Lord Himself appeared to them and convinced them that the Person communicating with them was identical with the Jesus they had known in the flesh. This they proclaimed across the world without doubt or hesitation. They spoke it when they knew it might cost them their lives to say it. They declared it with such power that the Christian church was born, became the new Israel of God, and was held together by continued personal experience with the living Christ. The results of the resurrection are the determinative facts of all history.

Do we have enough to sustain faith and to compel in us the same message? When we approach this study in prayer and faith, it becomes the most thrilling exploration of our lives!

The disciples knew Jesus. They were His friends.

They knew Him better than anybody else in the world. They had intimate association with Him day and night over a long period of time. They could not easily have been deceived as to His personality. From the point of view of acquaintanceship, they were the most competent witnesses to the personality of Jesus to be found anywhere in the world.

It is not making a profound judgment to invalidate their witness on the ground that they were not scientifically trained minds or that they did not apply criteria that some modern minds think they should have possessed. The criteria applicable to one age is not necessarily applicable to another age. The methodology of science is not necessarily the methodology of religion. Each has its own way to truth. The evidence which may satisfy critical minds of our century may be altogether unsatisfactory to those who live in subsequent centuries. To ask that all evidence of past happenings shall be able to stand the test of the age in which we live is to discount historical continuity, and to distrust all past historical revelations.

Dr. Hayes says, "The disciples may not have had the scientific frame of mind. They may not have been able in their day to sift and weigh evidence as we would sift and weigh it today. Truth may have been revealed to them in ways and by means which would not appeal to us, and which would not be likely to be the media employed for its revelation in the Occident and in the

twentieth century. Having made all the allowances for
all these things, we ask ourselves whether the disciples
were competent witnesses to the fact of the resurrection,
and if we free our minds from all religious and philo-
sophical presuppositions and simply listen to their testimony as that of honest and sensible men, we cannot
escape the conviction that the evidence offered them was
the best possible to their day and that their character
and their opportunities made them the most competent
witnesses which that age could furnish." [1]

The disciples were not fools. They were sensible, intelligent men. They were clear-eyed, clear-headed and
mature in their judgment. The Gospels and Epistles of
the New Testament emphasize that the disciples knew
just how the church had originated. They were unani-
mous in their opinion. They do not report hearsay evidence, vague gossip, hysterical or uncorroborated stories.
They tell us what they themselves saw and heard. They
were in fact the most competent judges of these things
to be found in the world at that time. They were not
prejudiced men. They were disposed toward criticism
rather than credulity.

When Mary Magdalene said she had seen the Lord
and when Cleophas and his companion came back from
Emmaus with their story, the disciples hesitated to believe it. The report was too incredible without further
experience. It seemed too good to be true. They were

ready to deny it. They were compelled to believe. Jesus showed them His hands and His feet. He convinced them by the most thoroughgoing experience that His identity was unmistakable. Thomas was given all the evidence his faith required.

The disciples were not easily brought to believe that the Lord had risen from the dead. At first, in prejudiced disbelief, they came step by step to make it an affirmation. This was accomplished by personal experience with the Lord Himself.

The quality of the disciples' lives made their testimony trustworthy. They were honest men. They taught men to live pure and holy lives. They were not trying to please the people, to be popular, to get a favorable hearing. They were good men who taught other men to be good. They were ready to risk everything for the privilege of preaching the truth. They lived holy, just and honorable lives. Their preaching had the note of sincerity. They were not frauds nor imposters. They rejoiced that they should count it worthy to suffer shame and martyrdom for the sake of Jesus.

Jesus hated hypocrisy. He could not live with sham and insincerity in religion. He said, "I am truth." He trained His disciples to be the servants of the truth. They could not be deceived and they were not deceivers. They were competent witnesses.

We are obliged to trust the testimony of the disciples

because of the kind of men they were and the kind of experience they report. They were good and honest men, reporting authentic personal experience.

They reported a variety of experiences from different points of view, testifying to the same central truth of the resurrection. They reported that the Lord appeared now to one alone and now to many. He appeared early in the morning and in the evening and at night. He came to them in a closed room, in the open garden, on the public road, in the private home, on the shore of the sea and on the mountain peak. He appeared in Jerusalem and in Galilee. He came to those who were convinced and to those who were doubting. He appeared to the expectant as though by appointment. He broke in upon those who were not expecting Him. He appeared to those who identified Him at once and to others who were slower in their perception. In most of the appearances He tarried long enough for conversation, instruction, encouragement. Under every variety of time and place and circumstance these disciples encountered the Lord. Their united testimony excludes the possibility of deception. These men were not deluded. Their testimonies checked and confirmed each other.

There could not have been collusion in their stories which could have held up through the years. Remorse would have driven someone to telling the truth; self-interest would have led another to betray the secret; torture would have compelled another to admit a prevarication. Men do not suffer for a delusion. Men do not die for a lie. The very simplicity, sincerity and directness of these men made their story irrefutable. They knew what they had seen. They told facts of their experience. They were honest men.

This was their message: "Christ is risen!" They made the declaration with all boldness and publicly at Pentecost fifty days after the crucifixion, while it was still possible to test every statement, to examine every witness, and to refute their testimony with any opposing facts. The apostles preached the resurrection to multitudes of people in the capital city at a great religious festival.

The reasons for accepting the testimony of these men are so overwhelming we are bound to hear their declarations as authentic and true. Five reasons make their testimony acceptable. They were the friends of Jesus. They were unprejudiced. They were honest in character. They could not tolerate a lie. They had every opportunity to get at the truth. The number of persons and the number and variety of experiences makes the news doubly sure. The gospel they preached was the gospel of the resurrection.

Paul had an encounter with the resurrected Christ at a later date than the other disciples, but his experience of the resurrection reality was for him authenticated in his own experience and verified by his own research. He spent some fifteen days with Peter and James and had an opportunity to perfect his knowledge on the subject of the resurrection. The written tradition, as reflected in the Epistle to the Corinthians, may go back as far as five years from the date of the resurrection itself. What Paul wrote about is the primitive and unbroken tradition coming from firsthand authorities such as Peter and James and Paul himself. Paul's first letter to the Corinthians antidates the gospel narratives by several years. Paul says that this is "the gospel which I preached unto you . . . and wherein ye stand . . . that Christ died for our sins according to the scriptures . . . and that he rose again the third day according to the scriptures: And that he was seen of Cephas, then of the twelve: After that, he was seen of above five hundred brethren at once; of whom the greater part remain unto this present, but some are fallen asleep. After that, he was seen of James; then of all the apostles. And last of all he was seen of me also, as of one born out of due time. For I am the least of the apostles. . . . But by the grace of God I am what I am . . . so we preach, and so ye believed." [2] This was indeed the gospel preached by the early church. It is the gospel which turned the world upside down. It is the gospel given to us to be preached. It is the only gospel of the Christian church. All other aspects of the life, teaching, death of Jesus derive their significance from this central truth.

If this gospel is a lie, it is the only lie to have blessed the years and survived the centuries with increasing power. If it is a lie, it is the only lie that has blessed, saved and redeemed man. If it is a lie, then all history is undependable and the church of Jesus Christ is the greatest fraud ever perpetrated. It cannot be a lie. It is inherently a declaration of God's wisdom, truth and power, authenticated in history and in personal experience.

Jesus Christ rose above life. He was not only separate from sinners but unique among saints. He was humanity's only impenitent saint. He is history's sinless exception.

Jesus Christ rose above sickness; until His last week there is no record of His being ill. He was whole and He was perfect. Healing went out of Him. His words were antiseptic. His deeds were remedial. Even His gestures carried healing in them.

Jesus Christ rose above falsehood. He stood up before men and asserted, "I am truth." Truth and His life were inseparable. One corroborated the other. He was truth. Every parable He uttered, every lesson He taught was an intellectual resurrection. He was truth incarnate.

Jesus Christ rose above death. His life was such a resurrection above other lives that death could not contain Him. In flesh and blood He was "Very God of Very God," as the Nicene Creed puts it. Being what He was, death could not defeat Him. We say it reverently! Anyone who was like Jesus and who lived like Jesus ought to have risen from the dead. Thank God, He did arise.

On a Good Friday morning, during a heavy action in

World War II, a young American soldier was severely wounded. He called for help and none came. He signaled to planes overhead but never got through. Finally, he dropped off into merciful unconsciousness. By and by a medical team picked him up. In a field hospital on Easter Day he regained consciousness. As his Chaplain stood over him that Easter morning, the young man said, "Chaplain, you can stand anything on Good Friday when you are certain of Easter Day."

That is the good news of the gospel! When you are certain of the resurrection you can stand anything. When you are certain of the resurrection you can have power, the power of the resurrection. When you are sure of the resurrection, you are sure of life. Christ is Risen! Christ is Risen! That is it. "Thanks be to God, which giveth us the victory through our Lord Jesus Christ." [3] That was the gospel of the apostle. And that is the only gospel given to the church to be preached.

9 The Word Everlasting

> "Lo, I am with you always. . . ." (Matthew 28:20, RSV)

> "And he led them out as far as to Bethany, and he lifted up his hands, and blessed them. And it came to pass, while he blessed them, he was parted from them and carried up into heaven. And they worshipped him, and returned to Jerusalem with great joy: And were continually in the temple, praising and blessing God." (Luke 24:50-53)

> "Jesus Christ [is] the same yesterday, and to day, and for ever." (Hebrews 13:8)

MANY AN AMERICAN soldier in World War II will remember the twin towns of Greenoch and Gorick on the Clyde River in Scotland. It was opposite these two cities that American troop ships cast anchor and discharged American combat forces for training centers throughout the United Kingdom.

107

But the town of Greenoch is renowned for other reasons. Here for a generation lived two very remarkable
men. One was a Covenanter minister named Strothers.
The other was a Free Church minister named Grant.
Their story has been portrayed in a little book, *Men of
the Knotted Heart,* the title of which is the Hebrew
idiom for "friendship." One chapter would speak of
Strothers, the other of Grant and the third chapter would
"knot" the two together. The book is a classic on enduring friendship.

They were men of extraordinary powers. James Denny
regarded Strothers as the most remarkable man in Scotland. He refused a Doctor of Divinity degree from Glas-
gow University; it was both costless and honorary, but
he felt it was unworthy of him to accept a degree he had
not earned. He was content with a small church and a
great life. He possessed a whimsical humor, was en-
dowed with intellectual superiority, and was a rock of
integrity in the land.

The two ministers belonged to a club to which they
went every Monday. Grant never entered the club without pausing with his hand on the door and whispering
something to himself. This private muttering occasioned
curious comment. One day Strothers was asked if he
knew what it was he said in this bizarre manner. "Yes,"
said Strothers, "I know what he says. He says, 'Christ is
risen.' " [1] That was Grant's way of keeping the central
fact of Christian faith in its central place. That was his

manner of keeping the chief theme of Christian theology and the central reality of Christian experience where it belonged. That was his way of keeping the daily events and common things of life under the supreme reality of Christian faith, the resurrection of Christ.

On that hilltop in Galilee, in the presence of a great host, our Lord promised to be with His followers forever. The closing verses of the Gospel of Luke and the first verses of the Book of Acts tell us that He met His disciples in the vicinity of Jerusalem for some final private instructions. Although they were Galileans whom the Judeans despised, they were commanded to tarry in Jerusalem. They were to declare what they had seen and heard. They were to know and interpret the Scriptures. They were to be reinforced in their lives and labors by the power of the Holy Spirit. There could be no doubt from this time on that Jesus was "declared to be the Son of God with power . . . by the resurrection from the dead," and that salvation could be preached in His name.

So Jesus went out of the sight of his disciples, and after Pentecostal power had come upon them, they went out to be witnesses of the things they had heard and seen. Twenty-nine times, in the Acts of the Apostles, it is recorded that they witnessed to the Lord's resurrection from the dead. They heralded the good news, the news commanded attention and produced conviction, and salvation by faith in Him followed. Witnessing to that

109

truth by word of mouth and by their holy living, the old Roman Empire, which was falling to pieces, was captured for the living Christ, and the famed Roman roads, built to be highways for the thundering legions of Caesar conquering more and more worlds, eventually (in the hidden, mysterious wisdom of God) were used not by the legionnaire but by the Christian apostle and missionary, marching in the name of the Nazarene.

That was the gospel then, and there is no other Christian gospel now. To amputate the resurrection fact, to diminish the resurrection experience from the gospel is to be left with something else than the Christian gospel. The incarnation, the resurrection, the ascension and the enduement with power are all the actions of the Eternal God and Father of our Lord Jesus Christ.

What Jesus Christ was once He is eternally. He went out of the sight of some men in order to be near to all men who accept Him forever. And to those who seek Him and find Him and know Him, He gives power. The author of the Book of Hebrews, in joyous exclamation, declares that "Jesus Christ [is] the same yesterday, and to day, and for ever."

Over and over again, for twenty centuries, the reality of the disciples' after-Easter experiences has been corroborated in the experiences of all who have come to Christ in faith. In every age He has been the same today as He was yesterday and will be forever. He keeps His promises. He is with us always.

He is the same today in forgiveness. Wherever He went and in whatever He did, He revealed God's mercy and forgiveness. Nobody was beyond the reach of the heavenly Father. God loved sinners so much that He was like a shepherd who, having one lost sheep, would leave the ninety-nine sheep secure in the fold to search for the one that was astray until that lost one was in safety, in the shepherd's loving care. So sinners would be salvaged, Jesus declared. That is the meaning of salvation.

A woman by a village well finds her tattered, tangled, sinful life restored to self-esteem and divine direction by drinking the water of life He offered. Another—accused of the basest sin and about to be pelted to death with stones—hears Him ask her accusers if they are free from sin. And when they do not answer, the accused one hears God's forgiveness, "Neither do I condemn thee: go, and sin no more." [2] To a rugged, calloused fisherman who had been alternately loyal and disloyal to Him, a man unstable, hot tempered and violent in action, He said, "Thou are Peter, and upon this rock I will build my church." [3]

Wherever the disciples went, they preached Jesus and His death upon the cross and His resurrection from the grave as the way to deliverance from sin. This was God's provision for forgiveness and renewal. "Repent and be baptized in the name of the Lord Jesus Christ." The fifth book of the New Testament, the Acts of the Apostles, is the story of conversions through the preaching of the apostles, who declared that our Lord is the Saviour from sin unto salvation and life eternal "by the resurrection from the dead."

Wherever the story of His wondrous love is told and men believe, forgiveness is experienced and new life follows. It is very simple, but it is the greatest of miracles. "God so loved that he gave his only Son, that whoever believes in him should not perish but have eternal life." [4] The missionary says it in a distant place. The Salvation Army says it on street corners, and at the penitent form men are redeemed by it. The church says it every week. "If we confess our sins, he is faithful and just, and will forgive our sins and cleanse us from all unrighteousness." [5] It happens in the open church, when during the week a lonely, agonizing soul bows down. It happens in a small group when a young man kneels at a chair and goes out cleansed, a man again—God's man for the rest of life. It happens in the ministers' studies; it happens in church pews. Wherever and whenever men and women and boys and girls come burdened with sin—confessing their need—He is the same in forgiveness. Old things pass away and all things become new. In His forgiveness He is the same today as He was yesterday and He will be forever.

And Christ is with us in His healing ministry. A lot of ridiculous things have been said and done in the name of healing through faith in Jesus Christ. But the fact is that He does bring healing and health. That was an apostolic accent and it is a contemporary reality.

Medical science now recognizes the reality of spiritual healing—not so much healing organic diseases, but in healing functional disorders. The whole development of psychosomatic medicine emphasizes the domination of what we call the spirit over the health of the body.

With Jesus the sequence of action was always first forgiveness, and then healing. You see them bring the sick to Him and He says, "Thy sins be forgiven thee . . . take up thy bed, and walk." [6] Forgiveness precedes healing, and it is a sound principle of the medical profession that a person whose life is clean, free from the vulgar, ugly, mean things that corrupt the nature and corrode the personality, is also a person free from fear and worry and more responsive to the healing process.

Direct divine healing is never a substitute for medical talent. The Christian employs all the best that medical science can provide, and then prays. Prayer reinforces the physicians and the technicians. Prayer brings peace of heart to the patient. Prayer takes out all the débris from life so that a liberated soul, an uncluttered mind, a free and whole personality may allow nature its full way.

The church has carried forward the commission of Jesus when He said that those who believed on Him should do yet greater works. Although healing antedates the Christian era, the church has been the mother of healing in the Christian era. Hospitals were originally hostels, way stations where pilgrims, especially those going to the holy land, stopped for physical and spiritual rehabilitation. The earliest doctors were monks and the nurses were nuns. It was the love of Christ in action which changed hostels into hospitals.

In West Africa a quarter of a century ago, a man lay on a hospital cot, still weak and helpless, but with new hope surging in his heart. He looked up into the seamed, haggard face of Dr. Albert Schweitzer and asked, "Who sent you?" The compassionate physician replied, "The Man of Nazareth sent me." He has been sending His healing into the world all these centuries.

And when we are sensitive to human suffering and the need for healing, and respond in love, the living Christ comes to help.

There came a time when I found myself in Old St. Louis Cathedral in New Orleans. I had gone, as so many visitors do, to that interesting church to admire the beautiful murals which were spread upon the walls by the artist who also painted the murals for the dome of our Nation's Capitol. Standing before the high altar, studying the art and the architecture, I was accosted by a curious little woman who fumbled and tugged at my sleeve. She wore the plainest calico dress. On her feet were sandals and a little black felt hat of Napoleonic form rested on her head. On her arm she carried a chip basket. "Please, sir," she pleaded, "can you tell me the name of the saint to whom I should pray in intercession for the healing of my eyes?" Then she proceeded to pour out a pitiful tale. She had been working for fifty cents a day, had developed cataracts and was taken to the charity hospital for the operation. She convalesced for some time and her vision seemed to improve. The hospital was so crowded she had to sleep on the floor. She had gone back to work for a while but was not earning enough for her food. Now, she said, "The shadows are returning again. Please sir, oh, please sir, tell me the name of the saint."

One could not remain untouched by such a tale. And turning to the woman I replied that I could not name the saint to whom she should pray, but that if she would pray to God through Christ, He would bend low to touch her and give her peace. So together, she a Roman Catholic and I a Presbyterian clergyman, knelt before the high altar of the church to ask Christ, the great Physician, to touch her. As we prayed, He came. With holy joy, a serene peace, and radiant countenance she arose and found her way out of the Cathedral. Do you think Jesus was real to me? I had gone to admire art, but because I had seen human suffering and felt Christ's adequacy to meet it, I came away with a living Christ in my own soul, walking the highway of life with Him as I had never known Him before. His illimitable grace had come down. He was alive and real to her and vivid to me at the point of human suffering.

And so He will come to us, any of us and all of us, when we respond in love and compassion to those who live in the shadow of poverty or ignorance, or in the world's concentrations of moral filth and human degradation, or suffer spiritual torment or physical illness.

Jesus Christ is our contemporary in His healing grace.

Jesus Christ is more than a dim figure in ancient history who must be saluted because of His rank. He is more than a celebrated person encased in ancient creeds and solemn declarations. He is our present friend and the companion of our days.

If Jesus Christ is to you only a beautiful character to be admired, or only a radiant mystic of unusual genius, or merely the master therapist who was the forerunner of modern psychiatry; or if you regard Him simply as a supreme teacher who laid the foundations of modern pedagogy—if these are the limits of your understanding of Jesus, then I have good news for you. There are fresh vistas and wondrous experiences of reality awaiting you. For Jesus Christ is alive, vivid to the consciousness, a real person who may be to you today what He was yesterday to Peter and James or John and Mary.

Jesus Christ is our contemporary in the work and worship of His church. He keeps His promise to be with His people wherever the gospel is truly preached and the sacraments faithfully administered.

He comes to us in the written Word.

Jesus Christ is alive in the Gospels. The prophets before Jesus and the rabbis of His time wrote books, but not so with Jesus. Jesus chose rather to write His life in men. Remade human beings were to be His copyrighted works and remodeled personalities were to be His new editions. He chose to make His inscription on the souls of men.

Some thirty to fifty years after the event at Calvary, when the eye witnesses began to die, a few of those who had walked with Him and had talked with those who had seen Him and had heard what He said, began to put down the life of the Master. These are only compilations of perhaps fragmentary episodes and instances from the story of the Nazarene, but after two thousand years they are more reliable historically than any other biographical sketch, because in them the essence of His being gets through to the generations.

Take one of these four sketches now called the Gospels, which is just about as long as an average serial story, and read it leisurely with an open mind at one sitting. See Him as the disciples saw Him, walking the dusty Palestinian highways, visiting the sick, comforting the bereaved, uttering imperishable words, proclaiming His enduring philosophy. Put down your New Testament and allow your mind to ruminate upon what you have read. You have something incredible; something which cannot be explained. Somehow He who knew what was in men then knows what is in men now. You are faced with a choice. Shall I seek Him and surrender to Him and find life, or shall I turn from Him and miss reality? Then, realizing your own need of Him and sensing that He does answer that need, in penitence, humility and faith, you give yourself to Him. Suddenly, you find Him! He appears. He is near. He is real. He is the same today as He was yesterday and will be forever.

Giovanni Papini relates that when he began his research in preparation for writing his monumental *Life of Christ,* he was not a Christian. But his study brought him through the sequences of experience from the Jesus of history to the living Christ. That was the only way Papini could understand Him. If He could come to Papini in historical research, He can come to us and He does come to us out of the Scriptures into the here and now.

He comes in ways we can understand.

One day we entered a sickroom. The young woman, brilliant in mind and radiant with the light of Christ, but unmindful of her serious malady, was crying for joy saying, "He's been here; He's been here." And for her He had been there. You may be sure of that. When she was gone, we picked up her Bible and found the clue to her testimony. A verse on a card prayed:

Lord Jesus, make Thyself to me
A living bright reality
More present to *faith's* vision keen,
Than any outward object seen.
More dear, more intimately nigh
Than e'en the closest earthly tie.

"More present to faith's vision keen, than any outward object seen," Ah, that is it! It is "faith's vision keen" by which He has remained the same today as He was yesterday and He will be forever.

He is with us in our worship at church. Whenever His people are joined in Common Worship—worshiping by common acts and united expressions—there is a Presence and a Power greater than the sum total of the individual participants. The Lord Jesus Christ is in the action. He comes in holy silences, He comes out of the written Word, He comes in the Word from the pulpit, He comes in hymns of praise, He comes in the at-one-ness of the people. There is in the action a Presence identifiable as the same Presence in the Upper Room in Jerusalem on Easter evening.

He comes to us through persons incandescent with His love and grace. Christ was and is the great universal Person. All humanity is in Him. He is many in one and One in many. He is a multitudinous Person. There was and will ever be only one Christ, eternally the same. He stands alone in His flawlessness. Only He was perfect among all the millions in all ages. Yet because He was and is the universal Person, He comes to men through individuals, imperfect in themselves, but with lives so kindled by His spirit that the living Christ is made known in them. One shows His manliness, another His kindness, another His sympathy, another His firmness, another His love, another His joy. In a mosaic of personalities, in a symphony of the spirit, He comes through some men to all men. "That reminds me of someone," we say. There are those persons, so much in Him and He in them, that all who meet them know that Christ lives.

One day John Wesley was preaching in the open air, as he did so often. People had gathered around him and were listening with eager attention to the sermon. On the outskirts of the crowd a gang of ruffians appeared. As they picked up stones with which to pelt the preacher, one of them called out, "Who is this man spoiling our fun?" "He ain't a man. Bill. He ain't a man!" another replied. Presently Wesley finished his message and the crowd parted respectfully to allow him to make his exit. As he got to the edge of the crowd he paused near the gang, and touching the leader on the head, said "God bless you, my man. God bless you." As that rough creature of the lower world looked up into the countenance of Wesley, he cried out, "He is a man, Bill! He's a man like God."

Over and over again men have looked into the faces of those who have walked with Christ and have discovered the living Lord drawing near.

Some time ago, a television show appeared called "The Brain-washing of John D. Hayes." I wish everybody could have known that man. For over forty years he was a missionary, supported by the gifts of the congregation I now serve. When the Japanese attacked Pearl

Harbor he was in China, and within a few days he and his family were arrested and interned. In due time his wife and children were returned to the United States, but John Hayes and his father were detained in camp. There he languished for over four years, suffering hunger and cold and disease. His father died and he buried him.

When the war was over, he came to Washington where he served as one of our assistant ministers and gradually rehabilitated his energies. He was loved dearly by everyone, but young adults and men in government service seemed especially fond of him. After several years he was restless to go back to China, where he was born and where he had served so long. Church officials at first declined to authorize his return because of the Nationalist-Communist conflict and because of the man's health. Dr. Hayes pleaded that he could handle the "Agrarian Reformers" if they would only let him go back. Eventually they sent him.

He saw Chiang's armies retreat and the Communists advance and establish themselves. At first the Communists allowed him to teach English in a city college, but forbade him to evangelize. The Communists had many urgent problems, but finally they got around to John Hayes.

In the middle of the night he was awakened and marched at bayonet point to prison—a dank, dark prison, without bed or normal personal facilities. From the cell he was taken intermittently during the day and at night and subjected to the awful ordeal of brain-washing. He was accused of being the leader of an American spy ring, although he was only a Christian missionary. They tortured him in spirit and in body. Five times they threatened to execute him. John Hayes said he determined to be true to truth and true to Christ. They weakened him, but they never broke him. We prayed for him, but had no word about him.

Then one day, for unexplained reasons, the Communists turned him loose and he made his way home. I shall never forget the Christmas Eve Communion service in which he officiated with me only a few days after his return. John Hayes still retained the beard he had grown in prison because the Communists allowed him no razor. This seemed to frame his countenance and emphasize his manliness. A young university student, an agnostic, sat with his relatives near the front of the church. The young man said, "I just couldn't keep my eyes off that face. Jesus Christ came through it." And He did.

For generations, in a benediction from the Scriptures, we have said, "The Lord make his face to shine upon you." Too often men have conceived God aloft with face "shining down" upon His people. But there is a deeper meaning. "The Lord make his face to shine upon you—upon your face." The Lord is to be in us and radiate through us.

In one of our great churches there served for a quarter of a century a wonderful minister. He was not the distinguished, eloquent preacher who occupied the pulpit and wrote books and poetry for the same number of years; he was the associate minister who called in the homes, visited the sick, counseled the troubled. He could preach well but did so very infrequently. In the service on Sundays he read the Scriptures or offered the prayer. He loved the people and the people loved him. In time they affectionately came to call him "Angel Face," so much did he show forth the compassion, the joy and the love of Christ.

One Sunday at dinner, following the service, the conversation of a family turned on the morning church service and a little boy in the family exclaimed, "Daddy, I smiled at God in church today and he smiled back at me!" To that little boy, James Leishman and Jesus had so lived together all these years that for that boy God and James Leishman were indistinguishable. So it has ever been. Men transformed by the love of Jesus Christ communicate His presence to others. That is why we need the church, where we encounter men who have encountered Him—and by their lives, the living Christ encounters us.

"Christ is risen" was the first good news. It has never ceased to be good news. For our Lord Jesus Christ is alive. Across the centuries there echoes the promise "I am with you always—even to the end of the end of the end. . . ." That is the kind of Christ we have. For Him we can live. In Him we can die. And in Him we shall live all the ages beyond death. He is here now, when we seek Him. He is here now, when we least expect Him. He will be with us in the grand climax of all time, for He is the same yesterday and today and forever.

"Behold, I stand at the door, and knock: if any man hear my voice, and open the door, I will come in to him, and will sup with him, and he with me." [7]

Notes

PREFACE

1. B. F. Westcott, *The Gospel of the Resurrection* (New York: The Macmillan Company, 1879), p. 300.

2. Alfred Edersheim, *Life and Times of Jesus the Messiah* (New York: Longmans, Green & Co., Inc., 1957), Vol. II, p. 629.

3. Richard Niebuhr, *Resurrection and Historical Reason* (New York: Charles Scribner's Sons, 1957), pp. 177, 181.

CHAPTER 1

1. John 20:15.
2. *Ibid.*
3. See John 20:17; Matthew 28:20.
4. Matthew 28:9, RSV.
5. Luke 24:39.
6. John 20:27.
7. John 20:18; Mark 16:10, 11.

CHAPTER 2

1. John 20:19; Luke 24:33.
2. Luke 24:34; I Corinthians 15:5.
3. Luke 24:39.
4. John 20:25, RSV.
5. John 20:27, RSV.

CHAPTER 3

1. John 20:29, rsv.
2. John 21:5, 6.
3. John 21:12, rsv.
4. Matthew 18:3.
5. Emily Dickinson, "The Child's Question."
6. Hebrews 13:5.
7. Matthew 28:20, rsv.

CHAPTER 4

1. So the record in Luke 24:34 and I Corinthians 15:5 suggests.
2. John 14:34, 35.

CHAPTER 5

1. Matthew 4:8, 9.
2. Luke 24:52.
3. Matthew 10:5.
4. Romans 1:4.
5. Edward Perronet.

CHAPTER 6

1. Luke 24:18, rsv.
2. Luke 24:19–21, rsv.
3. Luke 24:22–24, rsv.
4. Luke 24:25, rsv.
5. Luke 24:29, rsv.
6. Joseph Fort Newton, "The White Presence," in *God and the Golden Rule* (New York: Appleton-Century-Crofts, Inc., 1927).

CHAPTER 7

The view in this chapter has been expressed in several places, but nowhere more precisely and persuasively than in William M. Ramsay's *The Christ of the Earliest Christians* (Chapter 7) and in the Foreword of the book, written by James S. Stewart (John Knox Press, 1959).

1. I Thessalonians 1:9, 10, rsv.
2. John 20:30, rsv.

126

3. Acts 9:4, 5.
4. Philippians 3:10.
5. Romans 1:4.
6. W. J. Sparrow Simpson, *The Resurrection and Modern Thought* (New York, Longmans, Green & Co., Inc., 1911).
7. Doremus A. Hayes, *The Resurrection Fact* (Nashville, Cokesbury Press, 1932), p. 262.
8. Romans 10:9, 10, RSV.
9. Galatians 2:20.
10. Philippians 1:21.

CHAPTER 8

1. Hayes, *op. cit.*, p. 303.
2. I Corinthians 15:1, 3–11.
3. I Corinthians 15:57.

CHAPTER 9

1. Robert E. Speer, *Christian Realities* (Westwood, New Jersey, Fleming H. Revell Company, 1935), pp. 41, 42.
2. John 8:11.
3. Matthew 16:18.
4. John 3:16, RSV.
5. I John 1:9, RSV.
6. Mark 2:9.
7. Revelation 3:20.